FAITH CLINIC

VOLUME VII

- DIVORCE EDITION -

FROM "I DO," TO "BOY BYE!"

Finding God somewhere Between The Vows And The Court Date.

DR. PATRICIA S. TANNER

IBG
PUBLICATIONS
Putting the POWER in your pen!

Published by I.B.G. Publications, Inc., a Power to Wealth Company

Web address: www.ibgpublications.com

admin@ibgpublications.com / 904-419-9810

Copyright, 2025 by Patricia S. Tanner

IBG Publications, Inc., Jacksonville, FL

ISBN: 978-1-956266-95-5

Tanner, Patricia S.
Faith Clinic, Volume VII- Divorce Edition-Finding God Somewhere Between The Vows And The Court Date

Printed in the United States of America.

DEDICATION

To the silent seasons,
The unspoken griefs,
And the quiet strength that held us together.

This book is dedicated to every soul who has ever waited—
on healing, on closure, on God.
To the ones who have sat at their own bench of sorrow
and dared to hope again.

And most of all,
To the God who waited with me—
through silence, sorrow, and the search for meaning—
until I could rise again.

Your Faith Practitioner and friend,

DR. PATRICIA S. TANNER
The Faith Doctor

TABLE OF CONTENTS

INTRODUCTION

FROM, "I DO," TO "BOY BYE!"

Finding God Somewhere In Between The Vows And The Court Date

Let s start here: everything begins in the spirit before it ever shows up in the flesh. That fight you had over toothpaste caps and text messages? That wasn't just about toothpaste. It started in the unseen — the spirit. That's where God whispers, convicts, and tries to steer you before the crash.

But most of us? We wait until it manifests in the loud, messy, physical world before we admit something's broken.

Here s the kicker: for a lot of us, the marriage was spiritually over around year two. Yep, year two. You knew it. God probably tried to nudge you, but you hushed Him because, well, *the Bible says* or *my pastor told me to stay* or *my parents stuck it out for fifty years, so I should too.* So instead of listening to God in the spirit, you dragged twenty years of dead weight in the flesh — smiling in family photos while slowly bleeding out inside.

I get it. I did the same thing. I stuffed scriptures in my wounds like Band-Aids, but I wasn't healed. I listened to church folks say "God hates divorce" without realizing God also hates abuse, lies, idolatry, and betrayal. I made excuses. I wore a mask. And then, one day, the flesh caught up to what the spirit had been screaming all along: this was over, and pretending it wasn't was killing me.

The truth? Divorce doesn't start with lawyers and court dates — it starts when we ignore what the Spirit of God is showing us. **Galatians 5:16** says, *So I say, walk by the Spirit, and you will not gratify the desires of the flesh."* If we'd listened in the spirit, maybe we wouldn't have waited until our flesh — our emotions, our sanity, our finances — collapsed. But because we didn't, here we are.

And that's why I wrote this book. Not because I got it perfect, but because I didn't. I stayed too long. I confused endurance with obedience. I mistook cultural expectations for God's voice. I paid for it with wasted years, and I don't want you to. This isn't some "be strong and move on" pep talk. It's a clinic visit for your soul — sarcasm as the anesthesia, faith as the cure, and scripture as the prescription you can live on.

So, if you're ready to laugh at the mess, cry over the pain, and finally let God speak louder than your excuses, you're in the right place. From the vows to the court date, God has been there — not judging but guiding. And if you let Him, He'll take your "boy, bye" moment and turn it into the beginning of your *amen.*

So here we are. You swore on a stack of Bibles (or at least in front of Aunt Debra and the church choir) that it was *forever.* You said, "*I do,*" but life hit back with a very different script — and now you're standing in front of a judge whispering "boy, bye."

This wasn't the fairy tale, and let's be real, even Disney never warned us about child support payments and fighting over who gets the air fryer.

Divorce is messy. It's loud. It's painful. It's sarcastically funny in the "if I don't laugh, I'll cry into my pillow" kind of way. And if you're honest, you've probably wondered where God fits in all this. Is He shaking His head at your choices? Is He still in the room when your lawyer is quoting text messages you wish you'd deleted? Or did He ghost you the way your ex did?

Here's the truth — I've been there. I've wrestled with the questions, the paperwork, the shame, and the silence that follows when the vows are broken but your heart still beats. I had to claw my way through nights when forgiveness felt like a bad joke and mornings when hope felt like it didn't exist. And because I struggled, I created something to help you not drown the way I almost did.

This book isn't a self-help pamphlet. It's not a "10 easy steps to get over your ex" quick fix. Nope. This is a survival guide for the spiritually bruised and emotionally exhausted. It's the place where we'll peel back the glossy Instagram filters on marriage and admit the top reasons people really walk away — betrayal, money, silence, unmet expectations, and the list goes on. But more importantly, it's where you'll discover that God has not walked away from *you*.

So, buckle up. It's about to get raw, a little petty, uncomfortably honest, and very real. But stick with me — because somewhere between the "I do" and the "boy, bye," there's a God who refuses to let your story end in ruins.

Spoiler alert: He writes way better endings than divorce papers ever could. *Welcome to the Faith Clinic: Divorce Edition.*

I made it because I struggled — now you don't have to stay stuck like I did. Your appointment has already started. Don't worry — no co-pay required.

Faith Clinic Intake Form
Divorce Edition

Patient Name: _____

Date of Appointment: _____

Case Number (a.k.a. your ex's nickname): _____

Presenting Symptoms (Check all that apply):

☐ Still replaying the wedding video and wondering why you didn't trip at the altar.

☐ Can't say your ex's name without adding a creative insult.

☐ Using "God hates divorce" as your guilt blanket while secretly Googling divorce lawyers.

☐ Your prayer life sounds more like, "Lord, smite them," than "Thy will be done."

☐ Social media stalking that feels like part-time employment.

☐ Keeping the ring, but only because you're planning to sell it for vacation money.

☐ Wondering if Paul's "gift of singleness" comes with a return policy.

☐ Still at church pretending to be "happily married" while your spirit is screaming "help!"

Background Information:

- **Marriage Expiration Date (be honest — you knew):** Year _____ (while the divorce didn't happen until Year ____).

- **Top Reason for Marriage Death Certificate:**

  ☐ Infidelity (The side chick/preacher's kid/DM slide)

  ☐ Finances (a.k.a. Dave Ramsey was right)

  ☐ Communication breakdown (you stopped talking, but not yelling)

  ☐ Intimacy drought (Netflix > connection)

  ☐ Abuse (emotional, physical, or spiritual — not God's plan, by the way)

  ☐ Addiction (alcohol, porn, pills — or Amazon Prime packages showing up at the door)

  ☐ Unrealistic expectations (you thought it would be Ruth & Boaz, but got Samson & Delilah)

  ☐ Other: _____

Spiritual Vital Signs:

- **Prayer Pulse:** Weak ☐ Moderate ☐ Screaming at God in the car ☐

- **Faith Pressure:** Low ☐ High ☐ Fluctuates when the lawyer calls ☐

- **Hope Temperature:** Cold ☐ Lukewarm ☐ Fire shut up in my bones ☐

Immediate Care Needed: (circle all that apply)

☐ Healing from betrayal

☐ Strength to let go of dead weight

☐ Freedom from guilt disguised as scripture

☐ Grace to co-parent without homicide

☐ Faith to believe life isn't over after divorce

Doctor's Initial Note:

Patient presents with spiritual exhaustion, sarcasm as a coping mechanism, and a severe case of "stayed-too-long-itis."

Recommendation: Begin full treatment plan inside this book. Expect painful truths, heavy doses of scripture, and awkward laughter during recovery.

Prognosis: With God, healing is not just possible — it's promised.

Chapter 1

The Side Chick Wasn't In The Vows

💬 SYMPTOM:

⚕ THE BETRAYAL FACTOR

Infidelity. Cheating. Stepping out. Creeping. Sneaking. Whatever name you give it, the wound feels the same: gut-deep betrayal.

When you said, "*I do*," you weren't just promising to split bills and watch Netflix together. You were entering into covenant — the same heavy word God uses when He describes His relationship with His people. Covenant is supposed to mean, "I choose you, even when I don't like you." It's supposed to mean loyalty that doesn't check out when temptation checks in. But then it happens: the side chick, the late-night DM, the "she's just a friend" situation that turned into something else. And suddenly, covenant feels more like comedy — the cruel kind.

Infidelity isn't just physical. Let's get that straight. Some spouses never cross the hotel room threshold but have emotionally packed their bags years ago. Cheating can be emotional (texting someone more deeply than you talk to your spouse), digital (scrolling through half-dressed strangers on Instagram for hours), or even spiritual (sharing your soul with someone outside of your covenant while ignoring the one inside of it).

Jesus Himself said in **Matthew 5:28**, *But I tell you that anyone who looks at a woman lustfully has already committed adultery with her in his heart.*" Translation: you don't need a hotel receipt to qualify as unfaithful. Sometimes the biggest affair happens between the ears.

The symptom of infidelity hits like a flu you can't medicate away. It starts with suspicion — the late nights, the phone turned face down, the random "business trips" with no receipts. Then the confrontation: tears, anger, denial.

And finally, the truth: the person you trusted with your soul chose someone else with their body. That kind of betrayal doesn't just slice your marriage; it slices your sense of worth. You start asking: *Was I not enough? Was I too much? Did I miss God's voice when I married them? Or worse, did God set me up for this?*

And here's the sarcastic but honest part: everyone around you suddenly turns into a divorce expert. Some will say, "Girl, forgive and forget — God can restore!" Others will whisper, "Leave now — you deserve better!" Meanwhile, you're sitting in the middle of your living room floor wondering why forgiveness feels like swallowing broken glass and leaving feels like amputating your own heart.

The truth is, the symptom of betrayal doesn't just hurt your marriage — it contaminates your spirit. If unchecked, it turns into bitterness, and **Hebrews 12:15** warns us: *See to it that no one falls short of the grace of God and that no bitter root grows up to cause trouble and defile many."* Bitterness doesn't stay private. It leaks into friendships, into parenting, into how you see God Himself. It's like drinking poison and expecting your ex to die.

And yet, the symptom is real. Betrayal can make you want to shut down spiritually. Prayer feels pointless. Worship feels fake. You start side-eyeing happy couples in church like they're lying. And if we're honest, sometimes you want God to get them before He heals you. Sarcasm becomes your shield: "Oh, he cheated? Cute. Must be nice to be a man of *valor*," you mutter under your breath. Or "She's got him now — good luck paying those bills, sis." We joke to survive, but underneath, it's grief that doesn't have a funeral.

Here s where it gets raw: the marriage probably ended in the spirit long before the affair hit your flesh. That's the part no one likes to admit. The disconnection, the refusal to communicate, the neglect — it all showed up spiritually before it manifested as cheating physically. God likely tried to nudge you, whisper warnings, and stir conviction, but you pushed it aside because, hey, you were "in love" or "being faithful." The Spirit is always speaking before sin starts shouting. The problem is we didn't listen.

So, the symptom of betrayal? It isn't just about your ex. It's about the gap between what God showed you and what you chose to tolerate. And the sooner you admit that, the sooner healing begins.

Let's be real: betrayal doesn't just show up one random Thursday at 3:47 p.m. with a lipstick stain on a collar. It starts in the spirit. God always gives whispers before the storm. He doesn't blindside His children — but we often ignore His voice because it doesn't line up with what we *want* to hear.

Think about it. By year two, something had already felt off. The affection slowed down. The late-night conversations turned into late-night scrolling. Your spirit told you something was shifting, but you brushed it off because, well, "we just need counseling" or "marriage is hard for everyone." And yes, marriage *is* hard — but there's a difference between weathering storms together and living in a hurricane alone while your spouse is sending sunny selfies from someone else's phone.

The symptom of betrayal is this: your flesh experiences the pain, but your spirit saw it coming. God was dropping hints. The Spirit doesn't just shout in church; He nudges you at home. He's that uneasy feeling when you can't find peace around your spouse's story. He's that tug when you notice your own soul shrinking in a marriage that was supposed to bring life. But instead of listening, many of us doubled down. We quoted "God hates divorce" like it was a chain around our necks, not realizing that God also hates lies, betrayal, and covenant-breaking.

Here's where it gets sarcastically funny (or tragic, depending on the day): you stayed because other people had opinions. *"Well, my parents were married 50 years, so I will be too."* Cute. But were your parents happy, or were they just silent roommates? *"The Bible says stay."* Yes, but the Bible also says in **John 10:10** that Jesus came to give life, *life to the full.* How is hiding in your bathroom crying while your spouse is entertaining someone else giving you life to the full? Let's stop using scripture as duct tape to cover bullet holes.

The symptom of betrayal is more than the cheating itself — it's the disconnection from God's leading. By the time the affair happened, your spirit was already grieved. God was already trying to reroute you. Think about the Israelites: before Babylon came to drag them off, God sent prophets for *years*. He warned, He pleaded, He pointed. But they ignored Him until captivity knocked on their door. Betrayal works the same way. God whispers, *"Pay attention."* We say, "Nah, I got this." Then boom — we're in a courtroom, wondering where God was.

Spoiler: He was right there. He's been leading you from the start. The problem isn't that God didn't speak — it's that you didn't listen. **Proverbs 3:6** says, *"In all your ways acknowledge Him, and He will make straight your paths."* That includes your relationships. God will show you the cracks before they collapse the building, but we often ignore the warning because we're more afraid of looking like a failure than we are of disobeying God.

The symptom of infidelity also reveals how spiritual blindness turns into fleshly pain. When you don't discern in the spirit, you suffer in the flesh. By year two, God may have said, *"Pay attention."* By year ten, He may have whispered, *"You're dying here."* But you said, "I'll pray harder." By year twenty, you're signing divorce papers and realizing you confused *endurance* with *obedience.*

Here's the truth: betrayal isn't just a spouse breaking your heart. It's also a mirror showing you where you ignored God's heart. And that stings. But it's necessary. Because healing doesn't start with blaming your ex — it starts with admitting where you tuned out God's voice.

So yes, the side chick wasn't in the vows. But neither was bitterness, nor wasted decades, nor spiritual suffocation. Those didn't come from God — they came from ignoring God. The good news? He still leads. Even now, in the ashes.

Psalm 32:8 promises: *"I will instruct you and teach you in the way you should go; I will counsel you with my loving eye on you."* Betrayal doesn't silence God. If anything, it clears out the noise so you can finally hear Him again.

And maybe that's the ultimate symptom: not just the pain of being cheated on, but the regret of realizing God was speaking all along — and you get another chance to finally listen.

God s Covenant vs. Human Failure

Let's talk covenant.

Marriage isn't just a government-issued piece of paper. It's not just a joint mortgage and matching towels. Biblically, marriage is a covenant — a spiritual union that mirrors God's relationship with His people.

Ephesians 5:25 lays it out: *Husbands, love your wives, just as Christ loved the church and gave himself up for her."* Christ doesn't cheat. He doesn't slide into other DMs. He doesn't say, "Sorry babe, I found someone younger with fewer issues." He commits until the end.

But here s the issue: people aren't God. They fail. They fall. They choose sin over covenant. And when they do, the wound feels unbearable because you weren't just cheated on by a spouse — you were betrayed in the very thing that was supposed to reflect God's image.

Here s the faith truth: their failure does not cancel God's faithfulness. **2 Timothy 2:13** says, *If we are faithless, he remains faithful, for he cannot disown himself."* Your spouse may have walked out, but God didn't. The affair wasn't His stamp of disapproval on your life. The divorce papers weren't heaven's verdict against you. Humans betray, but God keeps covenant. That's the anchor you need to cling to when bitterness wants to drown you.

Now let's address the elephant in the church pew: *But doesn t the Bible say God hates divorce?"* Yes, **Malachi 2:16** says that. But let's look deeper. God hates divorce because it is violent to the soul — not because He wants you chained to abuse, betrayal, or spiritual death. He hates what divorce does to people, not the people who walk through it.

Jesus Himself made it clear in **Matthew 19:9** that marital unfaithfulness is grounds for release: *I tell you that anyone who divorces his wife, except for sexual immorality, and marries another woman commits adultery."* Translation: God is not oblivious to betrayal. He doesn't demand you stay in a covenant someone else already broke.

Here s another hard truth wrapped in sarcasm: some of us stayed decades longer than God ever asked us to. The marriage was spiritually over in year two, but you dragged it until year twenty.

Why? Because "the Bible says," or "what will people at church think?" Meanwhile, your spirit was suffocating while your flesh played dress-up.

That s not a covenant, that s captivity.

The teaching here is simple but not easy: God speaks in the spirit first. He shows you signs. He convicts. He reveals. But when you ignore Him long enough, what starts in the spirit eventually manifests in the flesh. The affair. The fight. The legal papers. And now here you are, asking God, "Why didn't You stop this?" when He's been trying to get your attention for years.

But here s the hope: betrayal is not the end of your story. **Romans 8:28** is still true, even when your ex is a liar: *And we know that in all things God works for the good of those who love him, who have been called according to his purpose."* Even this? Yes. Even the cheating. Even the divorce. Even the courtroom breakdown. God is not finished with you.

Healing after betrayal requires three things:

1. **Owning the reality** — Stop pretending it didn't happen. Betrayal broke you. Admit it.

2. **Rejecting false guilt** — You didn't make them cheat. That was their sin, not your responsibility.

3. **Returning to the Spirit** — Only in God's presence can your heart reset. Fleshly distractions (new relationships, petty revenge, or numbing addictions) won't heal you. Only His Spirit does.

Psalm 34:18 promises, *The Lord is close to the brokenhearted and saves those who are crushed in spirit."* Notice: He doesn't say He's close to the strong, the ones with perfect Instagram posts, or the ones who "forgave instantly." He's close to the broken. That means He's close to *you*.

So, let s land this: the side chick (or side dude) wasn't in the vows. They didn't promise to honor, cherish, and forsake all others. But God did promise to never leave you or forsake you (**Hebrews 13:5**). Their betrayal may have ended your marriage, but it didn't end God's covenant with you. That's the anchor. That's the hope. That's the teaching.

Here's the thing: marriage was never meant to be a glorified tax write- off or a cute wedding hashtag with matching T-shirts. It was designed to reflect God's covenant with His people. That's why betrayal hurts so deeply — because it takes something sacred and trashes it like last week's takeout. But let's cut through the Sunday school fluff. Humans stink at covenant. Always have. Always will.

Exhibit A: Israel. God rescued them from Egypt, gave them food that literally fell from the sky, parted seas, and still — still! — they cheated on Him with golden calves and other gods.

Exhibit B: Hosea. Hosea's entire ministry was one long painful sermon illustration: *"Hey Hosea, marry Gomer, a woman who will cheat on you repeatedly, so Israel knows how I feel when they chase idols."* (**Hosea 1:2**). That's the raw, ugly truth: betrayal isn't just a "modern problem." God has been dealing with spiritual side chicks since Genesis.

Here's where it gets real for us: your spouse's betrayal didn't surprise God. It broke your heart, but it didn't blindside His. And if anyone understands what it's like to be cheated on, it's God. He's the faithful husband who never strays, even while His people sneak around. **Jeremiah 3:20** says, *"But like a woman unfaithful to her husband, so you, Israel, have been unfaithful to me."* If you've been betrayed, you're in company with the very heart of God. He knows. He feels it. He's walked through it.

Now, here's the sarcastic kicker: sometimes, the betrayal wasn't the first problem. The spiritual disconnect was. Remember how we said the marriage was spiritually dead by year two, but you waited until year twenty to file papers? That's not faith, that's procrastination in holy clothing. We mistake endurance for obedience. We wear "long-suffering" like a badge of honor, when we're disobeying God by staying in what He already said was broken. It's like standing in a burning house, yelling, "But marriage is sacred!" while ignoring the fire alarm God Himself pulled.

Let's address the big, bold scripture everyone loves to throw in your face: *"God hates divorce"* (**Malachi 2:16**). True. But do you know what else He hates? Injustice. Oppression. Betrayal. Idolatry. Violence against the covenant He created. God hates divorce because it rips apart something He designed to be whole — but He also hates the lies and sin that made divorce the only sane option. In other words: stop weaponizing scripture to shame people into lifelong bondage.

And Jesus? He got it. In **Matthew 19:9**, He flat-out said that sexual immorality breaks the covenant. He wasn't giving free passes to every unhappy spouse; He was acknowledging the reality that betrayal already *ends* the covenant long before the paperwork does. Divorce doesn't break what's whole — it confirms what's already been fractured in the spirit.

What do we do with this? We learn the difference between God's covenant and human failure. God doesn't cheat. God doesn't lie. God doesn't leave you for someone younger or more "exciting." Humans might. But God's faithfulness is the anchor when people fail.

II Timothy 2:13 says, *"If we are faithless, He remains faithful, for He cannot disown Himself."* That means your ex's actions don't redefine your worth, your calling, or God's love for you.

Here's another sarcastic truth: staying in a dead marriage just because your parents did doesn't make you "holy." It makes you miserable. Let's stop idolizing endurance for endurance's sake. Your parents' marriage may have lasted fifty years, but if fifty years of silent resentment and spiritual suffocation is the goal, why bother quoting **Ephesians 5**? Covenant isn't just about time served — it's about life lived. Jesus came to give life *abundantly* (**John 10:10**), not "life-but-barely-breathing-because-my-marriage-is-a-prison."

Teaching moment: the Spirit always speaks before sin erupts. The affair didn't just happen. It was the fruit of a spiritual breakdown that started long ago. If we learn to tune into the Spirit, we'll stop tolerating what God already declared unhealthy. **Proverbs 3:6** isn't just a cute verse for graduation cards: *"In all your ways submit to Him, and He will make your paths straight."* That includes your marriage choices, your responses to betrayal, and even your decision to stay or go. When you submit to Him, He will lead you — even if it means leading you out.

But let's go deeper: betrayal has the potential to transform you spiritually, if you let it. **Romans 8:28** isn't just Christian bumper-sticker theology. It's raw reality. *"And we know that in all things God works for the good of those who love Him."* That includes betrayal. That includes divorce. That includes sitting in a courtroom feeling like you failed at life. God doesn't waste pain. He recycles it into purpose.

And maybe, just maybe, that's the lesson betrayal teaches best: people will fail you, but God won't. When the side chick (or side dude) takes what wasn't theirs, you're left standing with the One who never left you. Your ex might have broken the vows, but God didn't. That's where your healing starts — not with blaming them, but with rediscovering Him.

So, let's close this teaching with a blunt but freeing truth: divorce may have ended your marriage, but it didn't end your covenant with God. Betrayal may have shaken your confidence, but it didn't shake His throne. And the Spirit who tried to lead you before the breakdown? He's still leading you now — out of bitterness, into healing, and toward a future that isn't canceled just because your marriage was.

💊 FAITH PRESCRIPTION

*   **Daily Dose of Truth: Psalm 34:18** — *The Lord is close to the brokenhearted and saves those who are crushed in spirit."* Read it daily until your heart believes it.

*   **Forgiveness Capsules:** Slow release only. Forgiveness isn't instant, but it's freedom. Don't swallow bitterness — it only poisons you.

*   **Hope Injections: Romans 8:28**, as needed, especially when you feel abandoned.

*   **Boundaries Vitamins:** Build your immunity. Don't let the one who betrayed you keep access to your spirit. Pray for them, but keep the door locked.

🖌 HOLY SPIRIT CONSULT

Patient Note: " *God, I feel betrayed, abandoned, and humiliated. Did You leave me, too?* "

Holy Spirit Response: " *I was with you in year two, whispering. I was with you in year twenty, weeping. I didn't cheat — they did. I* *don t abandon My covenant. I am faithful. What they broke, I will rebuild. What wounded you, I will use to heal others. I am close to you now, closer than ever. You are not alone.*"

Scripture: Isaiah 61:3 — " *To bestow on them a crown of beauty instead of ashes, the oil of joy instead of mourning, and a garment of praise instead of a spirit of despair.*"

🙏 GUIDED PRAYER

Lord, I don t have polished prayers right now. I have broken ones. I feel betrayed and empty, but I thank You that You are close to the brokenhearted. Heal me where I ve been shattered. Teach me how to forgive without excusing sin. Protect my heart from bitterness. Remind me that Your covenant with me still stands, even if theirs didn t.

Thank You that You never leave or forsake me. I trust You to make beauty from ashes. Amen."

✴ DECLARATIONS

Say these until your spirit catches up with your mouth:

1. I am not defined by betrayal.
2. God's covenant with me is still intact.
3. What was meant to destroy me will develop me.
4. Forgiveness is my freedom, not my weakness.
5. Divorce didn't cancel my destiny. God is still writing my story.

Journal Reflection Page

- **When did I first sense in my spirit that my marriage was breaking before it broke in the flesh?**

_____

_____

_____

_____

_____

- **What lies about my worth have I believed because of betrayal?**

_____

_____

_____

_____

_____

_____

- **Where have I confused God's leading with people's pressure to stay?**

_____

_____

_____

_____

_____

_____

_____

_____

_____

• **Which scriptures give me strength when I feel most abandoned?**

_____

_____

_____

_____

_____

• **If I imagined life five years from now — healed, whole, and walking in freedom — what would it look like?**

_____

_____

_____

_____

_____

_____

_____

"God didn't authorize a third party in your covenant. When betrayal broke the bond, He saw the whole story— and He still stands with you in truth."

-DR. PATRICIA S. TANNER

Chapter 2

Broke People Argue Louder – And Pray Less

💬 SYMPTOM:

⚕ WHEN MONEY BECOMES THE THIRD PARTY

Let s be honest: you didn't think money would become the silent assassin in your marriage. You thought love would conquer all, that two people with big dreams and low bank accounts could "make it work." You thought the vows — *for richer or poorer"* — were romantic poetry, not a prophetic warning. And then reality showed up.

The bills came. The debt stacked. Someone lost a job. Someone else couldn't stop swiping the credit card like it was a magic wand. Suddenly, every conversation sounded like a budget meeting you didn't ask for. And instead of praying for provision, you started plotting arguments.

Money problems don't just strain a marriage; they choke it. They squeeze out intimacy, trust, and patience until all that's left is tension. It doesn't matter if you started off poor but hopeful, or wealthy but reckless. When financial stress enters, peace usually exits. And the symptom looks like this: you're no longer partners, you're opponents.

And let's sprinkle in sarcasm, because why not? Broke people fight over everything:

- *Why did you buy Starbucks when we re behind on rent?"*

- *Why did you forget to pay the light bill but remembered Amazon Prime?"*

- *Why is the tithe check late, but the PlayStation subscription auto-renewed?"*

It's not funny when you're living it — but looking back, sometimes you realize the fight wasn't about coffee or Netflix. It was about fear. Fear of not enough. Fear of failure. Fear of admitting you were both drowning financially and spiritually.

Here s the deeper symptom: money issues are never just about money. They're about trust — both with each other and with God. If we're honest, when the financial stress hits, prayer was the first thing to go. Instead of praying together, you argued louder. Instead of trusting God as Provider, you treated your spouse like the enemy. And over time, that broke more than the budget. It broke the bond.

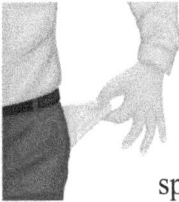 It's funny how nobody brings money to the altar, but somehow it always finds a seat in the front row of the marriage. You didn't exchange vows with a bank account, but over time, the balance sheet started talking louder than your spouse. The irony is that when you stood there on your wedding day, you probably promised "for richer or for poorer," not realizing that both "richer" and "poorer" would test you in ways love songs never warned you about.

Money, when left unchecked, becomes the third party you never intended to invite. Suddenly it's not you and your spouse against the world — it's you and your spouse fighting each other while money sits in the corner smirking like a homewrecker. And it doesn't take much to shift from "we're building a life together" to "we're blaming each other for bills, debt, and Amazon Prime deliveries."

Maybe it started small. One overdraft fee here, one late payment there. Maybe it was the innocent "I'll just use the credit card this one time" that became twenty times. Or maybe it was deeper: one spouse spends to soothe stress while the other saves to control fear. Suddenly every argument sounds like the same broken record: *Why did you buy that?" "Why didn t you tell me about this bill?" "Why is there never enough?"*

The truth is, money isn't neutral. It reveals what's in your heart. Jesus Himself said, *Where your treasure is, there your heart will be also"* (**Matthew 6:21**). And when hearts are misaligned about money, it's only a matter of time before bank statements become battlefield evidence. The symptom doesn't look like "we ran out of money" — lots of people are broke and still happy. No, the real symptom looks like:

- Silent resentment over who makes more.

- Constant nitpicking over who spends more.

- Power struggles over financial control.

- Secret spending that feels like betrayal.

- A lifestyle that looks good to outsiders but is drowning in debt behind closed doors.

And when the marriage counselor asks what went wrong, the couple shrugs and says, *irreconcilable differences."* Translation: *We let money become the referee, the scorekeeper, and the third party in our marriage."*

Money's power comes from fear. One spouse fears not having enough, so they hoard. The other fears not being enough, so they spend. Both think they're solving the problem, but they're just feeding the same beast. And the marriage becomes collateral damage.

But here's the kicker — money isn't even the real issue. The issue is what money exposed. Money doesn't lie; it tells the truth about your priorities, your trust in God, and your willingness to be one flesh. If the two of you can't get on the same page spiritually about money, don't be surprised when the marriage ledger falls into the red.

At the end of the day, "money fights" aren't about dollars. They're about dignity, trust, fear, and faith. And until those roots are confronted, money will always be the third party in your marriage, whispering lies, causing division, and making "irreconcilable differences" look like the only option left.

God s Wisdom On Money, Marriage, And Faith

The Bible talks about money a lot. Like, *a lot.* Over 2,000 verses address wealth, debt, greed, stewardship, and generosity. Why? Because God knew this would be one of the greatest tests of faith — and one of the top reasons marriages collapse.

Here s the thing: financial stress is real, but it doesn't have to be fatal. The real problem isn't the lack of money; it's the lack of alignment. **Amos 3:3** asks, *Do two walk together unless they have agreed to do so?"* If you and your spouse aren't on the same page about money, you're not walking together — you're dragging each other.

Money exposes what you really trust. Jesus said in **Matthew 6:21**, *For where your treasure is, there your heart will be also."* If your treasure is in appearances — keeping up with Instagram influencers, flexing with cars you can't afford — then your heart will live in debt. If your treasure is in fear — hoarding, withholding, never giving — then your heart will live in scarcity. And when hearts live in fear instead of faith, marriages suffocate.

Here s the sarcastic truth: some of y'all stayed in toxic marriages because you couldn't afford to leave. Love was gone, intimacy was gone, but that joint mortgage and car payment kept you chained together. You weren't covenant partners; you were financial roommates with legal paperwork.

God never intended money to be your master. **1 Timothy 6:10** says, *For the love of money is a root of all kinds of evil."* Notice it doesn't say money itself — but the love of it. Money becomes destructive when it rules you, when arguments about it drown out prayer, when finances become a bigger focus than faith.

So, what's the teaching here? **Money exposes your spiritual posture.**

- Do you trust God as Provider, or do you make your spouse the scapegoat for every financial fear?

- Do you steward what you have with wisdom, or do you let greed or recklessness run the show?

- Do you give generously, even in tight seasons, or do you hold back and wonder why nothing ever feels like enough?

Financial problems break marriages when couples ignore the spiritual side. Because everything starts in the spirit. If fear, greed, or selfishness lives in the spirit, then poverty, debt, and division will manifest in the flesh.

Here s biblical clarity: God provides. **Philippians 4:19** promises, *And my God will meet all your needs according to the riches of his glory in Christ Jesus."* That doesn't mean He funds your shopping sprees or covers bad stewardship. It means when you trust Him first, He aligns provision with purpose. But when you trust your spouse (or worse, yourself) more than Him, you will always feel broke — no matter what's in the bank.

And maybe that's the ultimate truth: financial betrayal (reckless spending, secret debt, withheld provision) isn't just about money. It's about covenant-breaking. It's a failure to honor God and each other with what He provided.

But here s hope: money doesn't have to be the death certificate of your future. Divorce may have ended the marriage, but it doesn't have to end your faith in God's provision. He is still Jehovah Jireh — the God who provides. And He provides not just for bills and groceries, but for healing, peace, and restoration.

Now let's shift from the symptom to the teaching — because God never leaves us stuck with just a diagnosis. He gives us a prescription. And when it comes to money, His wisdom has been on record long before Visa, MasterCard, or Sallie Mae came into the picture.

First, let s call it out plain: money is not evil. The Bible never said, *money is the root of all evil.* " What it actually says in **1 Timothy 6:10** is, *The **love** of money is the root of all kinds of evil."* Money is a tool. But like any tool, if it's mishandled, it can do damage. A hammer can build a house or break a window. Money can build a future or break a marriage. It all depends on how it's used — and, more importantly, whose wisdom you're following when you use it.

God's wisdom about money isn't just about budgets and spreadsheets. It's about trust. **Proverbs 3:9–10** says, *Honor the Lord with your wealth, with the first fruits of all your crops; then your barns will be filled to overflowing."* In other words, the very first conversation about money in a marriage should be: *How are we honoring God with what we have?"* Because when God is first, money loses its power to divide.

But here s the problem: most couples don't invite God into their money. They invite culture. Culture says, "Buy now, pay later." God says, "The borrower is slave to the lender" (**Proverbs 22:7**). Culture says, "Flex on Instagram." God says, "Be content with what you have" (**Hebrews 13:5**). Culture says, "Secure the bag." God says, "Seek first the kingdom" (**Matthew 6:33**). And marriages collapse not because the paycheck was too small, but because the wisdom guiding the paycheck was too shallow.

Another layer of God's wisdom on money and marriage is unity. **Genesis 2:24** says, *The two shall become one flesh."* That oneness doesn't skip over the wallet. If you're "one" in bed but divided in the bank account, you're living a partial oneness. And partial oneness always breeds hidden fractures. That doesn't mean you can't have separate spending accounts for convenience, but it does mean you can't treat money like it belongs more to one spouse than the other. Marriage is "ours," not "mine."

And yet, here s where faith comes in: unity with each other about money flows from unity with God about money. If both spouses don't anchor their financial life in faith, the marriage will always feel like tug-of-war. Because the spender isn't the problem. The saver isn't the problem. The income isn't even the problem. The real problem is whether both are leaning into God's wisdom, God's Word, and God's way of stewarding what He's entrusted.

So, what does that look like in practice? It looks like tithing when bills are screaming louder than faith. It looks like praying over decisions before signing on the dotted line. It looks like confessing financial mistakes to each other instead of hiding receipts in the glove compartment. It looks like building a lifestyle that matches God's provision, not Instagram's pressure. And it looks like reminding each other that provision comes from Jehovah Jireh, not from job titles, side hustles, or credit scores.

God's wisdom also calls us to generosity. Nothing crushes the spirit of greed and fear faster than giving. When a couple chooses to give — not recklessly, but faithfully — something shifts. Instead of seeing each other as financial enemies, you become partners in kingdom impact. You move from fighting over pennies to celebrating purpose. And suddenly money isn't the third party anymore — it's the shared testimony of how God can take two imperfect people and still provide more than enough.

And here s the truth that needs to land: money will always test your marriage, but it doesn't have to destroy it. Faith doesn't make money problems disappear, but it does give you a strategy that works in every season. Whether you're in the "richer" part or the "poorer" part of your vows, God's wisdom is the anchor that keeps you from drifting.

At the end of the day, the teaching is simple but not easy: stop letting money preach division in your house. Let God's Word preach unity. Stop seeing each other as opponents in the financial ring. See each other as partners in stewardship. Stop panicking over what you don't have and start praising for what God already gave. Because when money is dethroned and God is enthroned, marriage can breathe again.

⚕ FAITH PRESCRIPTION

- **Daily Dose of Truth: Philippians 4:19** — *And my God will meet all your needs according to the riches of his glory in Christ Jesus.*" Repeat this when fear of lack rises.

- **Budget Vitamins:** Stewardship isn't unspiritual. Start small: track, plan, and honor God with your money.

- **Generosity Drops:** Give, even when it feels hard. Generosity breaks greed's grip.

- **Peace Tonic:** Whenever anxiety about money flares up, pray together (even if it's just you now). Prayer invites peace where panic tries to live.

🌸 HOLY SPIRIT CONSULT

Patient's Note: *"Lord, I don't know how to move past all the fights over money. I feel like I lost years of peace, and I don't trust provision at all."*

Holy Spirit Response: *"I am your Provider, not your paycheck. I was faithful when manna fell in the wilderness, and I am faithful now. Money failed your marriage, but I will not fail you. Trust Me, and I will show you abundance that money can t buy: peace, joy, healing, and hope."*

Scripture: Matthew 6:33 — *But seek first his kingdom and his righteousness, and all these things will be given to you as well."*

🙏 GUIDED PRAYER

God, I confess that money has been my greatest fear and deepest wound. I let financial stress turn me against people I loved, and I let it choke out my faith. But I thank You that You are Jehovah Jireh, my Provider.

Heal me from fear. Teach me to trust You more than I trust numbers. Show me how to steward well and live in peace. Provide not just financially, but emotionally and spiritually, as I rebuild my life with You at the center. Amen."

✴ DECLARATIONS

Say these until your spirit catches up:

1. I trust God more than I trust money.

2. Lack does not define me; God's abundance does.

3. Financial stress will not control my peace.

4. I will steward what I have with wisdom and faith.

5. Divorce may have broken my finances, but God is still my Provider.

Journal Reflection Page

- **When did I first notice financial stress choking peace in my marriage?**

_____

_____

_____

_____

_____

_____

- **How did fear around money shape my choices and faith?**

_____

_____

_____

_____

_____

_____

_____

_____

- **Where did I ignore God's leading in financial decisions?**

_____

_____

_____

_____

_____

- **How can I reframe provision as God's responsibility, not mine alone?**

_____

_____

_____

_____

_____

- **If I believed Philippians 4:19 was absolutely true, how would I live differently today?**

_____

_____

_____

_____

_____

Chapter 3

Communication Or Confusion?

⚠ SYMPTOM

⚕ WHEN TALKING TURNS INTO TARGET PRACTICE

Let s be real: communication is the heartbeat of any relationship. Without it, marriages flatline. You started out talking for hours — texting good mornings, FaceTiming at midnight, finishing each other's sentences like a rom-com. Fast forward a few years, and suddenly the only thing you're finishing is each other's patience.

Here s the symptom: somewhere along the way, talking stopped being connection and started being combat. Words weren't bridges anymore; they were bullets. What used to be pillow talk became courtroom evidence. And instead of "I love you," it turned into "You always…" or "You never…" — followed by slammed doors, rolled eyes, and sarcastic claps.

Communication breakdown is one of the biggest silent killers of marriage. It doesn't always look like yelling — sometimes it looks like silence. The "silent treatment" feels like punishment dressed in maturity. But silence isn't holy; it's hostile.

Proverbs 18:21 says, *The tongue has the power of life and death, and those who love it will eat its fruit."* That means every word counts — spoken or withheld. If your marriage diet was built on sarcasm, avoidance, or bitterness, no wonder it starved.

And here's where it gets sarcastically sad: we'll spend more time talking to co-workers, friends, and even strangers online than to our spouse. You'll explain your day in detail to Karen at work but grunt "fine" at home. Or you'll write long posts on Facebook about "family life" while ignoring the person sitting next to you on the couch. That's not communication — that's public relations.

The symptom shows up like this:

- Arguments that loop back to the same old topics — finances, kids, in-laws — but never resolve.

- Conversations that start as "let's talk" but end with someone sleeping on the couch.

- Silent stretches that feel more like cold wars than peaceful pauses.

- Talking *at* each other instead of *to* each other.

Here s the kicker: many marriages don't end because of some big scandal like infidelity. They die from paper cuts of miscommunication, unspoken needs, and unresolved conflict. By the time divorce papers are filed, both people realize they haven't truly *talked* in years.

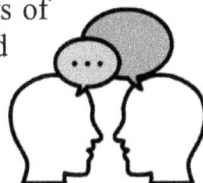

But deeper than that, communication failure starts in the ***spirit***. Everything does. Before your words got sharp in the flesh, your spirit was already disconnected. God leads by His Spirit, and when two people stop listening to Him, they eventually stop listening to each other. If prayer disappears from a marriage, conversation won't be far behind.

So, the symptom of "communication or confusion" isn't just yelling, nagging, or silence. It's the evidence of a deeper issue: both of you stopped hearing God, so you stopped hearing each other.

There's a difference between communication and combat. At the beginning of a relationship, words feel like gifts — every late-night conversation feels like a love letter, every text message feels like proof you've finally found "your person." But somewhere along the way, the tone shifts. Instead of words that build intimacy, the conversations become ammunition. What started as dialogue becomes target practice, with each spouse holding the other in the crosshairs.

It doesn't happen overnight. Nobody wakes up and says, *Today, I ll weaponize my words against the person I vowed to love."* But little by little, the disappointments stack up. Misunderstandings piled on top of unmet expectations, and soon words that were once tender start coming out sharp. You can feel it in the room — the sarcasm that isn't funny, the critique dressed up as "just being honest," the sighs that carry more weight than whole paragraphs. Suddenly, home doesn't sound safe anymore. It sounds like a shooting range.

And the thing about target practice is, no one aims for the air. Words hit flesh. They pierce. They wound. They linger. A cruel jab in the middle of an argument echoes long after the apologies. A dismissive tone becomes a silent poison that slowly drains affection.

Ephesians 4:29 tells us, *Do not let any unwholesome talk come out of your mouths, but only what is helpful for building others up."* But in marriages that are unraveling, words are rarely used to build anymore. They're used to break.

The symptoms look like this:

- Conversations that are once clarified now confuse.

- Arguments that start over something small turn nuclear because neither person feels heard.

- Silence that should bring peace instead becomes punishment.

- Every exchange feels like scorekeeping — who got the last word, who landed the deepest blow, who "won."

And here s the real danger: eventually, the words don't just attack the issue, they attack the identity. It's no longer *I m upset about what you did," it's *You always... You never... You re just like your mother... You re worthless."* And once words cross that line, they carve scars that last far longer than the argument itself.

Proverbs 18:21 says, *The tongue has the power of life and death, and those who love it will eat its fruit."* Too many marriages eat the bitter fruit of careless words, and by the time they sit in front of a counselor, their hearts are already riddled with bullet holes.

What makes this symptom so destructive is its subtlety. Money fights are obvious. Infidelity is glaring. But word wounds? They hide in plain sight. You can sit next to your spouse in church, sing the same worship song, smile for the same family picture, and nobody sees that behind closed doors, your marriage feels like a battlefield where "I love you" has been replaced by "I can't stand you." Talking turns into target practice when the goal of conversation shifts from connection to conquest. And left untreated, it doesn't just kill communication — it kills the marriage itself.

God s Blueprint For Words That Heal

Communication isn't just about words; it's about spirit. Jesus said in **Matthew 12:34**, *For the mouth speaks what the heart is full of."* Translation: if your marriage conversations are full of sarcasm, shouting, and shutdowns, it's because your hearts are full of hurt, pride, and fear. Words are fruit, not root.

The Bible doesn't treat words lightly. Proverbs is full of warnings about speech. **Proverbs 15:1** says, *A gentle answer turns away*

wrath, but a harsh word stirs up anger." Notice it doesn't say "the louder one wins." It says gentle words de-escalate conflict. But in most marriages, we picked volume over gentleness and then wondered why the house felt like a war zone.

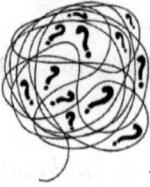

Let s call it out: many of us communicated better with strangers than with our spouse. Why? Because strangers don't hold our deepest wounds. Strangers don't remind us of unpaid bills or unwashed dishes. But your spouse? They're close enough to cut deep. And unless you let God heal your spirit, every conversation becomes an opportunity to wound instead of to build.

God designed marriage communication to mirror His communication with us. He speaks truth, but He also speaks love. He convicts, but He comforts. **John 16:13** promises, *But when he, the Spirit of truth, comes, he will guide you into all the truth.*" That means good communication in marriage starts with both people being guided by the Spirit of truth. Without Him, words get twisted into weapons.

Sarcastic truth time: half the arguments you had weren't even about what you were arguing about. You weren't fighting about the dishes — you were fighting about disrespect. You weren't mad about the thermostat — you were mad about control. The thermostat was just a prop in a bigger play called "We stopped hearing each other years ago."

And here s a brutal but freeing truth: when communication dies, intimacy follows. Marriages don't just collapse overnight; they erode in silence, sarcasm, and shouting until both people feel safer saying nothing than risking saying something. But here's God's design: communication should be life-giving, not life-taking.

Colossians 4:6 says, *Let your conversation be always full of grace, seasoned with salt, so that you may know how to answer everyone."* Grace should flavor our words, not bitterness.

Here s the teaching boiled down:

- **Words carry spirit.** What you say reflects what you believe.

- **Silence isn't golden if it kills connection.** Avoidance is not maturity.

- **Prayer is the first conversation.** If you stop talking to God together, you'll stop talking to each other.

- **God wants unity, not uniformity.** Communication isn't about agreeing on everything; it's about staying connected through everything.

So yes, communication breakdown may have ended your marriage. But God's blueprint for communication is still alive for you. He still wants to teach you how to speak truth with grace, how to listen with patience, and how to rebuild connection — with Him first, and eventually with others.

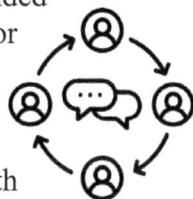

The good news is, God never leaves us to choke on the poison of broken communication. He gives us a blueprint — not just for avoiding harmful words, but for using words to heal, restore, and revive. The same tongue that can curse can also bless. The same lips that can tear down can also build up. And God's wisdom about words is clear: if you want a marriage that survives, you cannot speak death and expect life.

James 1:19 lays it out like a prescription: *Everyone should be quick to listen, slow to speak and slow to become angry."* Notice the order. Listening first, speaking second, anger last. But most marriages flip the order: quick to get angry, quick to speak, and almost never listening. The blueprint God gives us isn't about shutting down; it's about slowing down. Because healing words aren't rushed words. They're intentional, prayerful, Spirit-led words that aim to restore instead of destroying.

God's Word also teaches that what comes out of your mouth starts in your heart. **Luke 6:45** says, *For the mouth speaks what the heart is full of."* If your words are consistently harsh, resentful, or dismissive, it's not just a "communication problem," it's a heart problem. Healing begins not with better vocabulary, but with a transformed heart. When the Holy Spirit reshapes your heart with patience, grace, and humility, your words will follow.

So, what does this blueprint look like in action? It looks like spouses choosing to pause before launching verbal missiles. It looks like learning the discipline of speaking life even when emotions are running high. It looks like replacing *you always"* and *you never"* with *this hurt me"* and *I need us to work on this together."* It looks like swallowing pride long enough to apologize first. And it looks like creating a culture where encouragement is normal, not rare — where affirmations outweigh accusations.

Healing words don't mean avoiding hard conversations. They mean having them with the right posture. **Proverbs 15:1** reminds us, *A gentle answer turns away wrath, but a harsh word stirs up anger."* That doesn't mean sugarcoating truth, but it does mean delivering truth with love. It means tackling the issue without assassinating the person. It means remembering that the one across from you isn't your enemy — they're your partner, your covenant, your teammate.

And here's the spiritual depth: God Himself modeled what it means to use words that heal. From the beginning, He spoke life into chaos: *Let there be light."* He spoke comfort to the brokenhearted, correction to the prideful, and grace to the sinner. Jesus didn't walk around with verbal grenades.

He spoke words of restoration — words that lifted, convicted, and set people free. If the Son of God, who had every right to condemn, chose instead to speak healing, how much more should we — fragile, flawed humans — choose words that heal in our marriages?

Faith also reminds us that words aren't just about the moment — they're about legacy. Children overhear. Friends observe. Your spouse internalizes. Every sentence you drop becomes a seed. Healing words plant seeds of trust, intimacy, and resilience. Harsh words plant seeds of bitterness, resentment, and distance. And harvests always come.

The teaching is this: stop letting your tongue be a weapon in the enemy's hand and start letting it be an instrument in God's hand. Pray before you speak. Repent when you miss it. Build a rhythm of blessing instead of cursing. And when tension rises, remember — you're not just talking to a spouse; you're talking to God's son or daughter. That alone should change the tone.

At the end of the day, marriages don't fail because couples run out of things to say. They fail because they run out of words that heal. But God's blueprint is still available: choose life. Speak grace. Use words not as arrows to wound, but as bandages to mend. Because when your words align with God's wisdom, even the deepest wounds can begin to heal.

🔘 FAITH PRESCRIPTION

- **Daily Dose of Truth: Proverbs 18:21** — *The tongue has the power of life and death, and those who love it will eat its fruit."* Speak life, even when you feel death.

- **Listening Vitamins:** For every time you want to talk, practice listening twice as long. **James 1:19** — *Everyone should be quick to listen, slow to speak and slow to become angry."*

- **Prayer Capsules:** Pray out loud, even if it feels awkward. Invite God into your conversations.

- **Peace Tonic:** Before texting or talking to your ex (or anyone), ask: "Will these words heal, or will they harm?"

🦋 HOLY SPIRIT CONSULT

Patient Note:" Lord, I feel like my words don't matter anymore. I argued, I cried, I went silent. Nothing worked. Did You even hear me?"

Holy Spirit Response:" I heard every word. I caught every tear. Your words may have been ignored by them, but never by Me. I am still speaking to you — not in confusion, but in clarity. Let Me teach you how to use your voice for life again. The breakdown in your marriage doesn't mean your voice has no power. In Me, your words can still heal, encourage, and create peace."

Scripture: John 16:13 — *But when he, the Spirit of truth, comes, he will guide you into all the truth."*

🙏 GUIDED PRAYER

"Lord, I confess that my words haven't always brought life. I've yelled when I should have listened. I've stayed silent when I should have spoken truth. And I've used words as weapons instead of healing. Forgive me. Teach me to communicate with grace. Help me to listen to Your Spirit first, so that I can speak with love and wisdom. Heal the wounds left by words in my marriage and restore my confidence that my voice still matters. Amen."

✴ DECLARATIONS

1. My words carry life, not death.

2. I choose to listen before I lash out.

3. God still speaks to me, and I will listen.

4. Silence will not control me; wisdom will guide me.

5. Communication may have failed my marriage, but God will restore my voice.

📖 Journal Reflection Page

- **When did communication in my marriage begin to shift from connection to combat?**

_____

_____

_____

_____

- How did silence or shouting shape the health of the relationship?

_____

_____

_____

_____

- Where did I ignore the Spirit's guidance in how I spoke or listened?

_____

_____

_____

_____

- How can I practice hearing God first before speaking to others?

_____

_____

_____

- What would it look like to rebuild my voice as one that speaks life?

_____

_____

_____

Chapter 4

Sexless But Still Roommates

⚠ SYMPTOM:

🩺 WHEN INTIMACY CHECKS OUT, BUT THE LEASE REMAINS

Let's be honest — no one stood at the altar imagining a marriage where sex becomes a biannual event, circled on the calendar like a dentist appointment. But here we are. The vows promised unity, passion, and "two becoming one flesh." Reality? Two becoming roommates who share bills, chores, and maybe a Netflix password, but not much else.

Here s the symptom: intimacy has left the building. Oh sure, you still occupy the same space. The laundry gets folded, the kids get carpooled, the trash goes out on Tuesday. But the marriage bed? Cold. The touch that once felt electric now feels foreign, or worse, non-existent. You start realizing you've had more contact with your phone charger than with your spouse.

And it's not just about sex. Intimacy is broader — it's about connection, vulnerability, and safety. When intimacy goes silent, so does laughter, so does comfort, so does partnership. You start living parallel lives under one roof, like co-workers who tolerate each other for the paycheck. The house is occupied, but the covenant feels abandoned.

Here s the sarcastic truth: some marriages stay technically intact because of the mortgage, not the passion. Couples justify it with, *At least we re not fighting,"* as if silence equals peace. But in reality, it's just distance disguised as maturity. The bed may still be shared, but hearts are in separate rooms.

The symptoms look like this:

- "We're too tired" becomes the permanent excuse.

- One person feels rejected, the other feels pressured.

- Affection gets replaced by obligation.

- Porn, fantasies, or distractions sneak in to fill the void.

- Conversations about sex feel more awkward than discussing taxes with the IRS.

And deep down, your spirit feels it. Everything starts there. The Spirit knows when love has been replaced by duty, when covenant has turned into contract. You sense the absence of intimacy long before the flesh acknowledges it. You feel it in the distance, in the avoidance, in the way your soul is no longer nourished by your spouse.

But instead of dealing with it, you rationalize. *This is just what happens after a few years."* Or, *At least we're staying faithful."* Meanwhile, Song of Solomon is collecting dust on the shelf, and you're wondering why you feel more like a babysitter than a beloved.

The symptom of sexless marriages isn't just lack of pleasure — it's the slow suffocation of covenant. And by the time divorce papers are filed, the body simply caught up to what the spirit had been screaming for years: *we stopped being one flesh a long time ago.*

One of the clearest signs that a marriage is on life support is when the lights are still on, the bills are still getting paid, and both people technically still live under the same roof — but intimacy has long since packed its bags. On paper, the couple looks married. They may even sit side by side at church, sign Christmas cards together, and keep up appearances for the children. But behind the closed doors of that house, what was once a covenant feels like a cold cohabitation.

It's not always about sex, though physical distance is often the most obvious symptom. Intimacy goes deeper — it's the shared laughter, the random late-night conversations, the small touches, the eye contact that says, "I see you." When intimacy checks out, you feel it in the silence. Two people can sit inches away from each other on a couch and feel like they're worlds apart. Meals become transactions. "Good morning" and "goodnight" sound like courtesy, not connection. The house is full of noise — kids, television, chores — but empty of soul-level closeness.

This symptom can creep in quietly. Maybe life got busy: careers, kids, stress. Maybe conflict piled up, and every fight left another wall standing between you. Maybe betrayal shattered trust, and even after forgiveness, the distance lingered. Or maybe apathy settled in, and neither person fought to keep the flame alive. However it happened, the result is the same: intimacy leaves, but the lease remains. And that's the danger. Because marriages don't collapse only from shouting matches or scandalous headlines. Sometimes they die from quiet neglect.

Song of Solomon paints love as a blazing fire, but fire doesn't always go out because of a storm. Sometimes it dies simply because nobody bothered to tend it. Intimacy that isn't nurtured will eventually fade, and when it does, marriage becomes nothing more than two roommates sharing an address.

The pain of this symptom is brutal. You can be surrounded by people and still feel alone. You can technically "have a spouse" and yet ache like you're single. You may even find yourself fantasizing about escape, not necessarily because of someone else, but simply because you're starving for closeness.

Genesis 2:18 says, *"It is not good for the man to be alone."* But what happens when you're married and still feel alone? That's when hearts start wandering, temptations grow louder, and the covenant begins to unravel.

The silent tragedy is that couples living in this state often convince themselves it's fine. "We're not fighting." "We still pay the bills." "At least the kids are okay." But peace without intimacy is not peace. It's resignation. It's surviving but not thriving. And left untreated, it's a slow death sentence to a marriage that God designed to be alive, joyful, and connected.

God s Design For Intimacy

Let's clear something up: God invented sex. Not the devil, not Hollywood, not your ex with bad excuses. God Himself. **Genesis 2:24** says, *That is why a man leaves his father and mother and is united to his wife, and they become one flesh."* This wasn't just about surviving together — it was about thriving together, body and soul. Intimacy is holy.

Sex in marriage is more than a physical act. It's spiritual glue. It's vulnerability, trust, joy, and covenant made tangible. That's why Paul wrote in **1 Corinthians 7:5**, *Do not deprive each other except perhaps by mutual consent and for a time, so that you may devote yourselves to prayer. Then come together again so that Satan will not tempt you because of your lack of self-control."* Translation: intimacy is a shield against temptation, and when it disappears, doors open that were never supposed to open.

But here s the reality: when intimacy dies, it doesn't just kill sex — it kills connection. Marriages that become "sexless but still roommates" lose the spark that God intended to keep them bonded. And in that void, the enemy whispers lies:

- *You deserve better."*

- *At least porn doesn t reject you."*

- *Maybe someone else will appreciate you."*

And because the spirit was already disconnected, the flesh goes looking for substitutes. That's how affairs, addictions, and emotional entanglements sneak in.

But let's get brutally honest — sometimes the lack of intimacy isn't physical but spiritual. Couples stop praying together, stop worshipping together, stop being spiritually naked before God and each other. By the time sex disappears, the real disconnect started years earlier in the spirit. Because when you stop being one in the Spirit, eventually you stop being one in the flesh.

Here s the sarcastic truth: too many marriages quote **Ephesians 5** about wives submitting and husbands loving sacrificially but skip over the bedroom verse in **1 Corinthians 7**. You can't demand covenant benefits while refusing covenant responsibilities. You can't call yourself "one flesh" if the only thing you share is a Wi-Fi password.

God s blueprint for intimacy is this: it's sacred, it's mutual, it's holy, and it's life-giving. Song of Solomon doesn't read like a tax document — it reads like passion on fire. God designed intimacy to keep marriages alive, not just legally intact.

So, here s the teaching boiled down:

- **Intimacy is spiritual before it's physical.** When your spirit disconnects, your body will follow.

- **Sex is covenant glue.** Without it, temptation finds cracks to crawl through.

- **God doesn't want roommates.** He wants marriages that reflect passion, vulnerability, and joy.

- **Divorce started somewhere.** Divorce often starts in the bedroom of silence long before it ends in the courtroom.

But here's the hope: even if intimacy was lost, God can restore connection. **Psalm 147:3** says, *He heals the brokenhearted and binds up their wounds."* That includes wounds of rejection, neglect, and distance. Divorce may have exposed what was already gone, but God's healing can restore your spirit, your identity, and eventually your capacity for healthy intimacy again.

The good news is that intimacy doesn't have to stay checked out. God, in His wisdom, designed intimacy as a cornerstone of marriage — not as a bonus feature, but as a core necessity. From the very beginning, His design wasn't simply for man and woman to cohabitate. It was for them to be "one flesh" (**Genesis 2:24**). That's more than physical union. It's emotional, spiritual, and relational connection woven together.

God's design for intimacy is rooted in His own nature. He is relational — Father, Son, and Spirit in perfect unity. When He created marriage, He mirrored His own relational essence. That's why intimacy is not optional in marriage; it's essential. Without it, the covenant loses one of its primary purposes. Intimacy is where vulnerability meets safety. It's where flaws are exposed but still embraced. It's where two people experience a glimpse of God's covenant love — unconditional, sacrificial, and life-giving.

Scripture teaches us that intimacy flows from self-giving love. **Ephesians 5:25** calls husbands to love their wives as Christ loved the church — and how did Christ love? By giving Himself up. Intimacy thrives when both spouses choose sacrifice over selfishness, pursuit over passivity, and connection over convenience. It's not just about physical closeness but about creating an environment where the heart feels safe enough to open.

Healing this area requires intentionality. Couples can't assume intimacy will magically return just because they want it. They must choose to rebuild it. That might mean hard conversations about unmet needs, counseling to rebuild trust, or simply small daily acts of affection that say, "*I still see you.*" Intimacy often reignites not with a grand romantic gesture but with consistent small ones — a kind word, a lingering touch, undistracted attention.

And yes, physical intimacy matters. Paul reminds us in **1 Corinthians 7:3–5** that spouses should not deprive each other, except by mutual consent for a time of prayer. Why? Because physical intimacy protects against temptation and fosters unity. But it's not about obligation; it's about mutual care. God designed intimacy as a gift, not a chore. It's meant to refresh, reconnect, and reinforce the covenant.

Spiritual intimacy is equally vital. Praying together, reading the Word, worshipping side by side, creates a depth of unity that transcends surface-level connection. A couple can have physical passion but still feel empty if they lack spiritual connection. But when intimacy is anchored in God, it becomes resilient. Even when life gets stressful, that spiritual bond holds the couple together.

Ultimately, God's design for intimacy is about reflecting His covenant love. It's not mechanical. It's not transactional. It's not temporary. It's a living, breathing connection that requires attention, grace, and pursuit. And the best part? Even if intimacy has long checked out, God specializes in resurrections. The same God who breathed life into dry bones can breathe life back into a marriage where intimacy has gone cold.

🔖 FAITH PRESCRIPTION

- **Daily Dose of Truth: 1 Corinthians 7:5 —** *Do not deprive each other… then come together again so that Satan will not tempt you.*" Remember: intimacy is God's protection, not an option.

- **Affection Vitamins:** Learn to express love in small ways again — a word, a gesture, a prayer. Start in the spirit, let it flow to the flesh.

- **Vulnerability Drops:** Journal your feelings before God first, then allow Him to restore your openness with others.

- **Healing Tonic:** Ask God to break lies of rejection and replace them with His truth: you are desired, loved, and chosen.

🕊 HOLY SPIRIT CONSULT

Patient Note: "Lord, I feel abandoned in my own marriage. I felt more like a roommate than a spouse. Did I matter? Was I not enough?"

Holy Spirit Response:" You were always enough. Intimacy lost was not a reflection of your worth, but of a covenant gone neglected. I made you for connection, not rejection. I will restore your sense of being loved — not just by people, but by Me. You are seen. You are desired. You are Mine."

Scripture: **Isaiah 54:5 —** *For your Maker is your husband — the Lord Almighty is His name.*"

🙏 GUIDED PRAYER

"God, I confess that intimacy in my marriage became a wound I carried. I felt rejected, abandoned, unseen. But I thank You that You are the God who sees me and desires me.

Heal me where neglect broke me. Restore my confidence. Teach me to know that I am loved by You, even if I was unloved by them. And one day, teach me to build intimacy that reflects Your covenant, not brokenness. Amen."

✷ DECLARATIONS

1. I am desired, loved, and chosen by God.

2. Lack of intimacy does not define my worth.

3. God heals rejection and replaces it with connection.

4. I am not created to be a roommate — I am created for covenant.

5. My future relationships will reflect wholeness, not wounds.

📕 Journal Reflection Page

- **When did intimacy in my marriage begin to fade, and how did my spirit sense it first?**

_____

_____

_____

_____

_____

_____

- How did neglect in the flesh mirror disconnect in the spirit?

_____

_____

_____

_____

_____

_____

- What lies did I believe about my worth because of rejection?

_____

_____

_____

_____

_____

- Where is God inviting me to restore intimacy with Him first?

_____

_____

_____

_____

_____

_____

- **What would healthy, God-centered intimacy look like for me in the future?**

_____

_____

_____

_____

_____

_____

_____

_____

_____

_____

_____

_____

Chapter 5

Control Freaks, Manipulators, & The Holy Ghost Don't Mix

🗒 SYMPTOM

℞ WHEN LOVE TURNS INTO LEVERAGE

Control. It doesn't wear a neon sign, but you feel it tightening like a noose. What started as "I just care about you" slowly morphed into "Do it my way or else." Love shifted into leverage, and instead of partnership, you found yourself in a silent tug-of-war where only one person ever wins.

The symptom of a control-driven marriage looks like this:

- Every decision — from dinner plans to major life choices — gets filtered through their approval.

- Your voice gets smaller while theirs gets louder, until you don't recognize yourself anymore.

- Manipulation masquerades as love: *If you loved me, you d do this."*

- Spiritual abuse sneaks in: verses twisted like weapons to demand submission instead of partnership.

Control doesn't always scream. Sometimes it whispers in the form of guilt. *After everything I ve done for you, you can t even...?"* Or it parades as concern: *I just know what s best for us."* But at its root, control suffocates love, because love without freedom isn't love — it's bondage.

And here s the sarcastic reality: marriages ruled by control feel less like a covenant and more like working for a very cranky boss. You're not a spouse; you're an employee expected to clock in, follow orders, and not talk back. And if you do? Prepare for punishment — cold shoulders, withheld affection, or maybe a well-timed Bible verse about submission.

Here s the deeper truth: the spirit senses control before the flesh feels it. The Holy Spirit is about freedom (**2 Corinthians 3:17** — *Where the Spirit of the Lord is, there is freedom.*") When your marriage feels more like a prison than a partnership, your spirit knows something's off. But instead of trusting that nudge, many stay, quoting "sacrifice" while silently suffocating.

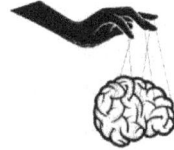

The symptom of control leaves you anxious, walking on eggshells, rehearsing conversations in your head to avoid conflict. And over time, you lose the very identity God gave you. Instead of reflecting Christ's image, you reflect their demands. That's not covenant — that's captivity dressed in a wedding band.

One of the most heartbreaking shifts in a marriage is when love, once free and generous, morphs into leverage — a tool for control. Love was never meant to be a bargaining chip, yet in broken relationships it becomes weaponized. "If you loved me, you'd do this." "Until you change, I won't give you that." Affection turns conditional, apologies become currency, and every act of care feels transactional instead of heartfelt.

When love becomes leverage, the relationship stops feeling like a covenant and starts feeling like a contract — a long list of if/then clauses. Instead of freely given grace, each spouse begins keeping score. One cooks dinner and expects repayment through intimacy. One buys a gift and expects obedience in return. One withholds affection until the other complies. Slowly, the marriage stops being a safe place and becomes a prison where both are inmates, walking on eggshells and calculating their moves to avoid emotional punishment.

The tragedy is that many couples mistake this symptom for "normal" marriage tension. Society tells us relationships are all about compromise, about "meeting in the middle." While compromise is sometimes necessary, when it turns into leverage, it is no longer love — it's manipulation. Love gives without strings. Leverage attaches a price tag. The difference is subtle at first, but the damage is deep.

For example, a wife might withhold words of encouragement until her husband meets her expectations at work. Or a husband might withdraw affection until his wife conforms to his idea of respect. In each case, love is twisted into a tool of control. Over time, intimacy suffocates under the weight of unspoken contracts.

The pain of this symptom is multilayered. For the person being manipulated, it feels like nothing they do is enough. They begin living under constant performance pressure, striving to "earn" affection instead of resting in unconditional love. For the one doing the leveraging, they often don't realize the harm they're causing. They may believe they're "motivating change" or "holding their spouse accountable," but really, they're eroding trust.

And trust is the foundation of intimacy. Without it, the covenant starts to rot. Scripture tells us in **1 Corinthians 13** that love "keeps no record of wrongs." But when love turns into leverage, records are not only kept — they're weaponized. Arguments become courtrooms where past failures are dragged up as evidence, and forgiveness is held hostage until demands are met.

What makes this symptom so dangerous is that it often masquerades as strength. "I'm just setting boundaries." "I'm just protecting myself." But in reality, it's a distortion of boundaries into barriers. True boundaries guard the marriage from harm. Leverage manipulates the marriage for control. Love is no longer given as a reflection of God's covenant but as a conditional reward, and when that happens, the marriage begins to feel less like a union and more like a prison sentence.

God s Blueprint For Partnership, Not Prison

Let s clear something up: God designed marriage as partnership, not dictatorship. **Genesis 2:18** says, *It is not good for the man to be alone. I will make a helper suitable for him."* Helper doesn't mean servant. It means partner, counterpart, equal in worth, designed to walk side by side.

The Hebrew word for "helper" — *ezer* — is also used to describe God Himself as Israel's helper. So, if you think "helper" means doormat, you're already twisting the text.

Control-driven marriages completely miss God's blueprint. **Ephesians 5:21** says, *Submit to one another out of reverence for Christ."* Mutual submission. Not one person ruling while the other shrinks. Not manipulation disguised as leadership. Mutual. Submission.

Manipulation thrives where truth is absent. That's why Jesus said in **John 8:32**, *Then you will know the truth, and the truth will set you free."* If your marriage left you in bondage, constantly questioning your sanity, constantly shrinking to keep the peace — that wasn't truth. That wasn't freedom. That wasn't God.

Here s the sarcastic truth: some people turn scripture into shackles. They weaponize "wives submit" while conveniently forgetting "husbands love your wives as Christ loved the church and gave

Himself up for her" (**Ephesians 5:25**). Spoiler: Jesus didn't manipulate the church. He didn't gaslight her. He didn't guilt-trip her. He sacrificed for her. If submission in marriage looks like slavery, it's not biblical. It's abuse dressed in Christianese.

Control and the Holy Ghost don't mix because the Spirit is about freedom, choice, and love. Manipulation violates all three. Love, by definition, requires freedom. Anything else is coercion. And God doesn't coerce — He invites.

Revelation 3:20 shows Jesus knocking, not barging in. He respects boundaries. He honors free will. If your marriage felt like constant invasion and coercion, know this: that was not God's design.

Let s also be real: control isn't always one-sided. Sometimes both spouses play tug-of-war. One controls finances, the other controls intimacy. One manipulates with guilt, the other manipulates with silence. Either way, the covenant gets twisted into a power struggle. And a marriage where no one truly yields to the Spirit will always end in collapse.

Here s the teaching boiled down:

- **Marriage is partnership, not prison.** God designed equality, not hierarchy.

- **Manipulation is a spirit — and it's not holy.** It comes to steal identity, silence voices, and kill covenant.

- **Freedom is God's standard.** If it doesn't look like freedom, it's not God.

- **Divorce often reveals where control already killed love.** The papers just confirm what the Spirit already grieved.

But here s hope: even if control defined your marriage, God restores freedom. **Galatians 5:1** says, *It is for freedom that Christ has set us free. Stand firm, then, and do not let yourselves be burdened again by a yoke of slavery."* Divorce may have ended the marriage, but it doesn't have to end your freedom. The Spirit is still leading you out of bondage, back into identity, and forward into peace.

God never designed marriage to be a place of control, fear, or manipulation. His blueprint was always partnership. From the very beginning, in **Genesis 2:18**, God declared, *It is not good for the man to be alone. I will make a helper suitable for him."* That word "helper" is not about servitude — it's about strength. The Hebrew word *ezer* is used elsewhere in Scripture to describe God Himself as a helper to Israel. In other words, the wife was never meant to be a pawn or possession, but a powerful partner.

Partnership means shared responsibility, mutual honor, and covenant love that reflects Christ's relationship with the church. In **Ephesians 5**, Paul paints the picture of marriage as mutual submission — *Submit to one another out of reverence for Christ"* (**Ephesians 5:21**). This isn't about leverage. It's about humility. It's about each spouse seeking the good of the other, not seeking control over the other.

God's design for love is freedom, not coercion. Love thrives in an atmosphere where both partners feel safe to be themselves, flaws and all, without fear of rejection or manipulation. Where leverage keeps a spouse in bondage, partnership sets them free. **Galatians 5:13** reminds us, *Do not use your freedom to indulge the flesh; rather, serve one another humbly in love."* That's the essence of biblical marriage: serving, not leveraging.

When a marriage follows God's blueprint, love is not earned — it's given. Grace flows freely. Forgiveness is extended even when it isn't deserved. Sacrifice is made not as a transaction but as an act of devotion. Partnership says, "We're on the same team." Prison says, "You owe me." One reflects Christ. The other reflects the world.

To break free from the symptom of love-as-leverage, couples must repent of using love as a weapon and return to God's design. That means letting go of scorekeeping and embracing forgiveness. It means refusing to withhold affection as punishment. It means learning to communicate needs honestly without manipulation.

For example, instead of saying, "If you loved me, you'd do this," a partner might say, "When this happens, I feel unseen. Can we work together on this?" One is leverage. The other is partnership. One tears down trust. The other builds it.

Couples must also invite God into their intimacy. Alone, human love is limited and easily corrupted by selfishness. But when anchored in Christ, love becomes resilient, selfless, and enduring. Jesus modeled covenant love by laying down His life for us — not because we deserved it, but because He chose us. That is the love He calls spouses to mirror in marriage.

Finally, we must remember that marriage is not a prison. Christ came to set us free, not to put us in chains. When love feels like leverage, it is a sign that something has strayed from God's design. But His grace redeems. What was once manipulation can become mutual honor. What was once a prison can become a partnership. And what was once leverage can once again become love.

FAITH PRESCRIPTION

- **Daily Dose of Truth: 2 Corinthians 3:17** — *Where the Spirit of the Lord is, there is freedom."* Memorize this until freedom feels natural again.

- **Boundary Vitamins:** Practice saying "no" without guilt. Freedom requires boundaries.

- **Truth Capsules:** Call manipulation what it is. Lies lose power when exposed to truth.

- **Freedom Tonic:** Daily invite the Holy Spirit to remind you of your worth and identity.

HOLY SPIRIT CONSULT

Patient Note:" Lord, I felt trapped. My voice didn't matter, my

choices didn't matter. I felt like a prisoner, not a partner. Where were You?"

Holy Spirit Response:" I was whispering freedom while you were enduring captivity. I never asked you to shrink to stay married. I never asked you to tolerate manipulation in My name. I designed you for freedom, not bondage. You are Mine, and your worth is not tied to their control. Walk with Me — I will restore your voice and your identity."

Scripture: Galatians 5:1 — *It is for freedom that Christ has set us free."*

GUIDED PRAYER

"God, I confess that I stayed silent when I should have spoken, and I allowed control to suffocate me. Forgive me for confusing endurance with obedience. Heal me from manipulation's lies. Restore my voice, my freedom, and my identity. Thank You that the Holy Spirit lives in me, and where Your Spirit is, there is freedom. Teach me to walk in that freedom daily. Amen."

✳ DECLARATIONS

1. I am not a prisoner — I am God's child, created for freedom.

2. Manipulation has no authority over my life.

3. My voice matters, because God gave it to me.

4. I will not confuse endurance with obedience again.

5. Where the Spirit of the Lord is, I walk in freedom.

📓 Journal Reflection Page

- **Where did I first feel the Spirit warning me about control in my marriage?**

_____

_____

_____

_____

_____

_____

- **How did manipulation shape my identity and silence my voice?**

_____

_____

_____

_____

_____

_____

- **What lies did I believe that kept me in captivity?**

_____

_____

_____

_____

_____

_____

- **How does Galatians 5:1 speak to my current season of freedom?**

_____

_____

_____

_____

_____

- **What practical boundaries can I put in place to protect my freedom moving forward?**

_____

_____

_____

"You can't control what you won't surrender. Manipulation is not a fruit of the Spirit— and the Holy Ghost doesn't play tug-of-war with pride."

-DR. PATRICIA S. TANNER

Chapter 6

Addiction Was The Third Partner In The Marriage

📋 SYMPTOM

℞ WHEN YOUR SPOUSE MARRIED THEIR HABIT TOO

Marriage was supposed to be a duet, but it felt more like a trio — you, them, and their addiction. You didn't sign up for this unwanted roommate, but somewhere along the way, it moved in. Addiction doesn't knock politely; it barges through the door and demands space at the dinner table, the bedroom, and the bank account.

At first, maybe you brushed it off. *Everyone has a vice."* Or, *It s just stress."* Maybe you excused it with, *They ll grow out of it."* But addictions don't grow out — they grow roots. And soon enough, you realized you weren't competing with another person, but with a bottle, a pill, a screen, or even a paycheck.

The symptom shows up like this:

- Trust disintegrates. You never know if they're sober, lying, or covering up.

- Finances crumble — money vanishes into bottles, online subscriptions, or reckless binges.

- Intimacy disappears — you can't compete with whatever "comfort" they've chose.

- Promises mean nothing — every apology sounds like déjà vu.

- Your spirit feels drained — you're carrying weight God never asked you to carry.

Addiction doesn't just affect the addict — it drags the whole household into chaos. You start living in a cycle of hope, disappointment, forgiveness, relapse, repeat. And sarcastically speaking, you could write your own rehab manual just from experience:

✓ **Step 1**: Believe their apology.

✓ **Step 2**: Watch them relapse.

✓ **Step 3**: Cry into your pillow.

✓ **Step 4**: Repeat until your sanity collapses.

And here s the deeper layer: the Spirit was whispering all along. You knew. The late nights, the missing money, the glassy eyes — your spirit recognized the intruder before your mind admitted it. But instead of heeding God's warnings, you drowned them out with excuses. And year after year, the addiction became the loudest voice in the marriage, silencing love, trust, and peace.

The real symptom? Addiction creates idolatry. It dethrones God in the marriage and enthrones a substance, a screen, or a habit. And idolatry always destroys covenant. By the time divorce papers are filed, the addiction has already eaten away at everything sacred.

Some marriages don't just include two people. They include a third party — and no, not another lover, but a habit that refuses to leave. Maybe it's alcohol. Maybe it's gambling. Maybe it's pornography, spending, lying, or workaholism. Habits can be silent roommates in a marriage, taking up space, eating away at intimacy, and demanding loyalty from the one who is supposed to be devoted to their spouse.

When your spouse marries their habit too, you often feel like you're competing for their affection. Their addiction, their obsession, or their coping mechanism becomes the mistress that never leaves. The sting of betrayal cuts deep, even if the habit isn't another person. Because the truth is, anything that takes the attention, devotion, and energy that should belong to a spouse becomes an idol — and idols destroy intimacy.

For the spouse watching it happen, the emotional toll is crushing. You may feel invisible, replaced, or discarded. You may question your worth, wondering why your partner would choose a bottle, a screen, or a behavior over you. Nights get lonelier, conversations feel shallower, and the marriage slowly begins to suffocate under the weight of something that doesn't belong.

And for the spouse trapped in the habit, there's often a mix of shame and denial. They may know the habit is killing the marriage, but they don't know how to stop. The habit becomes a prison cell, and they're both inmate and jailer. They defend it one minute and hate themselves for it the next. They may promise change, but without deliverance, the cycle repeats: apologies, false starts, relapses, tears, and more apologies.

 The pain of this symptom is that it doesn't just create distance — it creates division. Trust begins to crumble. Faith in the relationship begins to fade. The home that was meant to be a refuge becomes a battlefield of silence, suspicion, and sorrow. What should be a partnership begins to feel like a tug-of-war between the spouse and the habit.

Worse yet, many Christian couples downplay this symptom, excusing it with "everybody struggles with something." While it's true that we all wrestle with weakness, bondage is not the same as weakness. Habits that become masters over us aren't just struggles

— they're chains. And chains don't just weigh down one spouse. They drag down the entire marriage.

This symptom forces a hard truth to the surface: you can't be fully present in a marriage if you're fully devoted to a habit that owns you. You can't cling to your covenant and your chains at the same time. Eventually, one will win. And when the habit wins, the marriage loses.

God s View On Bondage & Freedom

Let s not sugarcoat it: addiction is bondage. **John 8:34** says, *Very truly I tell you, everyone who sins is a slave to sin."* Addiction enslaves. It strips away freedom, identity, and intimacy. And when one spouse is enslaved, the other is collateral damage.

God never designed marriage to include bondage. He called it partnership, covenant, and freedom. **2 Corinthians 3:17** declares, *Where the Spirit of the Lord is, there is freedom."* So, when addiction rules a house, it's clear the Spirit isn't allowed to lead.

Here s the sarcastic truth: some Christians hide behind spiritual excuses. *Oh, it s just my thorn in the flesh."* No, Paul's thorn didn't come in a bottle or on a website at 2 a.m. *God understands my stress."* Sure, He does — that's why He said, *Cast your cares on Me,"* not, *Drown them in tequila."* Addiction is not God's comfort; it's counterfeit comfort.

Marriage with addiction feels like being unequally yoked even when you share the same last name. **Amos 3:3** asks, *Do two walk together unless they have agreed to do so?"* You can't walk in unity when one spouse is walking with God, and the other is walking with Jack Daniels, pills, or porn tabs. Addiction breaks alignment. And where alignment is broken, covenant crumbles.

Now let's talk about the other side — the spouse trying to hold it together. You prayed, cried, forgave, and begged God to heal them. And maybe He did for a while, but the relapse came. And each time, a piece of your trust broke off until you were left with nothing but shattered faith. Hear this clearly: you didn't fail. You weren't unloving or unspiritual because you couldn't "save" them. Only Jesus saves. You are not the Holy Spirit.

Biblically, addiction is often described as idolatry. **Romans 6:16** says, *Don t you know that when you offer yourselves to someone as obedient slaves, you are slaves of the one you obey—whether you are slaves to sin, which leads to death, or to obedience, which leads to righteousness?"* Addiction is slavery, and it brings death to joy, peace, and eventually marriages. Divorce doesn't create the death — it simply acknowledges what addiction already killed.

But here s the good news: God's specialty is freedom. **John 8:36** says, *If the Son sets you free, you will be free indeed."* That includes freedom from the shame of staying too long, freedom from guilt over walking away, and freedom from the lie that addiction disqualified you from God's love.

Here s the teaching boiled down:

- **Addiction enslaves; God frees.** The two cannot coexist in covenant.

- **You are not their savior.** Stop confusing your love with God's Lordship.

- **Divorce doesn't cancel your worth.** Addiction broke the covenant; papers just sealed the reality.

• **God redeems even this.** Freedom is still available — for them, if they choose, and for you, no matter what.

God's heart has never been for His children to live in bondage. From Genesis to Revelation, His story is one of setting captives free. The Exodus shows us a God who doesn't leave His people in slavery. The cross shows us a Savior who breaks the chains of sin. The resurrection shows us that death itself couldn't keep Him bound. Freedom is not just God's preference for His people — it's His promise.

Romans 6:16 reminds us, *Don t you know that when you offer yourselves to someone as obedient slaves, you are slaves of the one you obey—whether you are slaves to sin, which leads to death, or to obedience, which leads to righteousness?"* God makes it plain: we are either bound to sin or bound to Him. There is no neutral ground. When a spouse is bound to a habit, it means their loyalty is divided. That divided loyalty damages not only their walk with God but also their marriage.

God's blueprint for marriage was never designed to include bondage. **Ephesians 5** compares the relationship between husband and wife to the relationship between Christ and the church — a covenant of sacrificial love and freedom. Christ doesn't bind His bride with chains of addiction. He liberates her with grace. In the same way, spouses are called to walk in freedom so that their love can reflect God's design.

Bondage in marriage isn't just about personal sin — it's spiritual warfare. The enemy loves to use habits as strongholds because they choke out intimacy, sow mistrust, and distract couples from their kingdom purpose. **John 10:10** says the thief comes to steal, kill, and destroy, and habits that become masters accomplish all three. They steal time, kill trust, and destroy

intimacy. But Jesus declared, *I have come that they may have life, and have it to the full."* That's freedom.

The pathway to freedom begins with surrender. No spouse can rescue their partner from bondage by themselves. You cannot out-love an addiction. You cannot out-argue a habit. Freedom comes only when the person bound surrenders to Christ, the only chain-breaker. That doesn't mean the other spouse is powerless — prayer, boundaries, and support matter deeply — but it does mean we must recognize the difference between playing Savior and pointing to the Savior.

Practically, this looks like honesty over denial. It looks like confession over secrecy. It looks like accountability over isolation. **James 5:16** says, *Confess your sins to each other and pray for each other so that you may be healed."* Healing comes not by hiding the habit but by dragging it into the light.

For the spouse on the receiving end of their partner's bondage, God's wisdom is this: love them, pray for them, but do not enable them. Enabling is not the same as grace. Grace empowers change. Enabling excuses destruction. Boundaries, counseling, and spiritual guidance may be necessary, not as acts of rejection but as acts of love. Because true love does not allow a spouse to drown in chains while pretending everything is fine.

God's view of freedom is holistic. He doesn't just want individuals free — He wants marriages free. He wants households marked not by bondage but by blessing. **Psalm 128** paints the picture: a home where God's presence fills the atmosphere, where joy and fruitfulness flow from the covenant. That kind of marriage cannot thrive where habits hold the keys.

The good news is this: bondage doesn't have to be the end of the story. What looks like defeat can become a testimony of deliverance. Habits that once ruled can be broken. Spouses who once felt enslaved can walk in freedom. Marriages that once felt hopeless can be resurrected. Because the same God who split the Red Sea, who opened prison doors for Paul and Silas, who rolled away the stone on Easter morning — that God is still breaking chains today.

If your marriage feels like it's being strangled by a habit, hear this: God's design is freedom. His power is greater than any addiction. His grace is stronger than any bondage. And His plan for your marriage is not for you to live as inmates, chained to cycles of defeat, but as partners walking hand in hand in the liberty Christ purchased on the cross.

💊 FAITH PRESCRIPTION

- **Daily Dose of Truth: John 8:36** — *So if the Son sets you free, you will be free indeed."* Declare this over yourself daily.

- **Release Capsules:** Write down what burdens you carried for them that were never yours to carry. Hand them back to God.

- **Identity Vitamins:** Remember: you are not the addiction, and you are not defined by their choices.

- **Hope Tonic:** Keep believing God heals, but don't confuse His ability with your responsibility.

🕊 HOLY SPIRIT CONSULT

Patient Note: "Lord, I felt like I was married to their addiction, not to them. I tried everything, but nothing worked. Did I fail?"

Holy Spirit Response: "You did not fail. You loved, you prayed, you carried — but freedom is a choice only they could make. Addiction was their idol, not your identity. I never asked you to be their savior. That role is Mine alone. I am still your healer, your provider, and your peace. Walk free in Me."

Scripture: Romans 6:14 — *For sin shall no longer be your master, because you are not under the law, but under grace."*

🙏 GUIDED PRAYER

Lord, I confess that addiction wounded my marriage and my spirit. I tried to carry what was never mine to carry. I release that burden to You. Heal me from guilt, rejection, and anger. Remind me that You alone set captives free. Restore my peace. Redeem my story. Teach me to trust Your freedom more than their failures. Amen."

✸ DECLARATIONS

1. Addiction does not define me or my future.

2. I am free from guilt that was never mine to carry.

3. God redeems even what addiction destroyed.

4. My worth is intact, no matter their bondage.

5. Freedom is my inheritance in Christ.

📘 Journal Reflection Page

- **Where did I first notice addiction creeping into my marriage?**

_____

_____

_____

_____

_____

_____

_____

• **How did I try to carry their bondage as my burden?**

_____

_____

_____

_____

_____

• **What lies did I believe about my role in "fixing" them?**

_____

_____

_____

_____

_____

_____

- **How does John 8:36 speak to my identity today?**

_____

_____

_____

_____

_____

_____

_____

- **What does walking in true freedom with God look like for me?**

_____

_____

_____

_____

_____

_____

_____

_____

_____

Chapter 7

Growing Apart, Or Just Refusing To Grow Up?

▤ SYMPTOM

⚕ WHEN PETER PAN MARRIES, BUT NEVER PUTS AWAY TOYS

Let s be blunt: some marriages don't end because of betrayal, finances, or addictions. They end because one person grows up and the other clings to Neverland. What started out as "cute quirks" eventually morph into a 40-year-old tantrum you don't have the energy to babysit anymore.

The symptoms of immaturity in marriage are painfully obvious:

- They chase hobbies harder than responsibilities.

- They treat bills like suggestions, not obligations.

- They avoid conflict by sulking, ghosting, or running to mommy instead of facing reality.

- They want all the benefits of marriage — sex, companionship, security — without the responsibilities of commitment, sacrifice, and growth.

Immaturity doesn't just show up in behavior. It shows up in the spirit. **1 Corinthians 13:11** says, *When I was a child, I talked like a child, I thought like a child, I reasoned like a child. When I became a man, I put the ways of childhood behind me."* Some people said, "I do" at the altar but never said "I grew."

Here s the sarcastic reality: you thought you married a partner, but you really married a dependent. You didn't get a spouse; you got a second child. And then the church told you to "just pray harder," while you were secretly Googling parenting techniques to survive your marriage.

The Spirit always warns before the flesh collapses. By year two, you saw it: irresponsibility, tantrums, the refusal to evolve. But instead of listening to God's nudge, you said, *They ll mature eventually."* Twenty years later, you realize "eventually" never came. The real symptom? You didn't just grow apart — they refused to grow up.

And immaturity is contagious. It drags down the whole covenant. You can't build a kingdom when one partner is still playing in the sandbox. You can't build a life when one person keeps escaping into excuses. You can't carry the weight of marriage alone without breaking under it.

Every marriage begins with promises but promises are fragile when one spouse is still living like a teenager in an adult body. You probably know the "Peter Pan" type — the one who marries but never grows up. They're stuck in perpetual adolescence, clinging to hobbies, irresponsibility, or reckless habits that keep them from showing up as a real partner. They want the benefits of marriage — intimacy, companionship, someone to cook dinner and share bills with — but they refuse the responsibilities that come with it.

This symptom shows up in countless ways. Maybe it looks like a husband who works just enough to pay for video games but leaves his wife drowning in bills. Maybe it's a wife who spends hours scrolling social media and shopping online while neglecting the needs of her household. Maybe it's someone who runs back to their parents at every sign of conflict instead of facing issues head-on. Whatever the specific behavior, the root is the same: immaturity disguised as freedom.

And immaturity, unchecked, is not just annoying — it's dangerous. A spouse who refuses to grow up leaves their partner carrying the weight of two people. The "responsible one" becomes both parent and partner, shouldering emotional, financial, and spiritual burdens that were meant to be shared. Over time, resentment builds. Exhaustion sets in. What should feel like a partnership begins to feel like babysitting.

Even worse, perpetual immaturity stunts the marriage's spiritual growth. A spouse who clings to childish patterns avoids accountability, dodges correction, and resists sacrifice. They want love without labor, intimacy without investment, and covenant without commitment. And while marriage can survive many storms, it cannot thrive when one person is still pretending that life is a playground.

The Bible warns us about this kind of stagnation. Paul writes in **1 Corinthians 13:11**, *When I was a child, I talked like a child, I thought like a child, I reasoned like a child. When I became a man, I put the ways of childhood behind me."* A marriage stuck in perpetual immaturity is a marriage stuck in childhood reasoning. Arguments sound like playground fights. Conflicts are met with sulking instead of solutions. Decisions are avoided until they explode. And slowly, a home meant to reflect God's order begins to look more like a daycare of dysfunction.

This symptom doesn't just wound the spouse forced to "pick up the slack." It also cripples the one refusing to grow. Because while immaturity feels comfortable for a season, it robs them of the joy that only responsibility brings. Real manhood, real womanhood, real covenant living is not found in clinging to childish ways — it's found in growing into the roles God designed us for. And until growth happens, marriage will feel more like a lopsided contract than a covenant.

God Calls Us To Maturity, Not Perpetual Childhood

Let s talk truth: marriage requires growth. Not perfection, but progress. **Ephesians 4:15** says, *Instead, speaking the truth in love, we will grow to become in every respect the mature body of him who is the Head, that is, Christ."* God designed life to be a journey of maturity. You can't stay spiritually or emotionally stunted and expect covenant to survive.

Immaturity destroys marriages because it refuses responsibility. It avoids accountability. It rejects growth. But covenant demands the opposite — responsibility, accountability, and growth in love.

Let s go sarcastic here: immaturity looks like throwing a fit over dishes while ignoring the fact the mortgage is late. It looks like storming out of arguments instead of learning conflict resolution. It looks like playing video games for six hours while your spouse carries the household. And yes, hobbies aren't bad — but when your "me time" consistently tramples covenant time, immaturity rules.

Here's the bigger issue: immaturity is spiritual before it's practical. **Hebrews 5:12** scolds believers who should have been teachers but still needed milk: *Though by this time you ought to be teachers, you need someone to teach you the elementary truths of God s word all over again."* Spiritually immature people make immature spouses. They don't pray, they don't seek God, and then they wonder why their marriages collapse under the weight of real life.

God's blueprint is maturity. Growth is His expectation. You're not supposed to be the same person in year 20 as you were in year 2. **Romans 12:2** commands transformation: *Do not conform to the pattern of this world but be transformed by the renewing of your mind."* Transformation requires responsibility. Immaturity resists it.

Here s the truth: sometimes you didn't "grow apart" — you grew, they didn't. You matured spiritually, emotionally, and mentally. They stayed stuck in cycles, tantrums, and excuses. And eventually, the covenant broke not because you changed, but because they refused to.

But here s the hope: just because your marriage ended in immaturity doesn't mean your future is stunted. God matures those who walk with Him. **Philippians 1:6** promises, *He who began a good work in you will carry it on to completion until the day of Christ Jesus."* Your growth isn't wasted. Your maturity will outlive the marriage that couldn't handle it.

Here s the teaching boiled down:

- **Immaturity breaks covenant.** You can't build on sand.

- **Growth is spiritual first.** A stagnant spirit produces a stagnant marriage.

- **God calls us to put away childish ways.** Maturity is not optional — it's commanded.

- **Divorce doesn't cancel growth.** If anything, it exposes where it was resisted.

God has always called His people to grow. From Genesis to Revelation, maturity is not an option — it's the expectation. He doesn't save us so we can stay stuck. He saves us so we can grow into His likeness, reflect His character, and live out His purposes. And that includes maturity in marriage.

Hebrews 5:12–14 is blunt about this: *In fact, though by this time you ought to be teachers, you*

need someone to teach you the elementary truths of God s word all over again. You need milk, not solid food! ... But solid food is for the mature, who by constant use have trained themselves to distinguish good from evil. "

God doesn't want His children staying on spiritual baby formula forever. He calls us to grow up, and that includes how we love, how we communicate, how we handle money, and how we show up for our spouse.

Maturity in God's design is not about age but about responsibility. It's not about how many years you've been alive but about whether you are willing to carry what God entrusts to you. Marriage is one of those sacred trusts. **Ephesians 5** paints the picture of marriage as Christ and the Church — a relationship built on sacrifice, love, and spiritual depth. That cannot be fulfilled by spouses who refuse to grow.

Maturity means learning how to handle conflict without turning it into combat. It means making financial decisions with wisdom instead of impulse. It means putting aside selfish desires for the sake of the covenant. It means seeing intimacy not just as physical pleasure but as a reflection of unity. It means realizing that your spouse is not your parent, your toy, or your servant — they are your partner in purpose.

God doesn't shame us for immaturity, but He does call us out of it. **1 Corinthians 14:20** says, *Brothers and sisters, stop thinking like children. In regard to evil be infants, but in your thinking be adults. "* In other words: childishness is fine when it comes to sin — stay innocent. But in responsibility, thinking, and spiritual growth, we put away childish things.

The truth is that growth will always cost us comfort. It's easier to run from bills than to budget. It's easier to hide from hard conversations than to face them. It's easier to play than to pray. But God's call is not to easy — it's to maturity. Because only maturity produces the fruit that sustains a marriage. **Galatians 5:22–23** describes that fruit — love, joy, peace, patience, kindness, goodness, faithfulness, gentleness, and self-control. Immaturity produces the opposite — chaos, selfishness, and instability.

The good news is maturity is possible. You don't have to stay stuck in Peter Pan syndrome. God gives grace for growth. The Holy Spirit develops fruit in our lives when we surrender daily. And even if immaturity has wounded your marriage, healing can begin when one or both spouses choose to grow.

Marriage doesn't need perpetual children trying to play house. It needs adults who are willing to lean on God, learn from His Word, and live with responsibility. God's blueprint is not about robbing us of joy but about giving us the deep joy that only maturity can bring — joy that comes from building a covenant strong enough to last storms, trials, and temptations.

If immaturity has been the third party in your marriage, hear this truth: God is calling you higher. He's calling you out of childish ways and into the strength of adulthood. He's calling you to trade toys for tools, selfishness for sacrifice, excuses for growth. Because maturity is not just the expectation of marriage — it's the evidence of faith. And when spouses grow up together in Christ, their marriage becomes not a playground of dysfunction but a garden of fruit that lasts.

💊 FAITH PRESCRIPTION

- **Daily Dose of Truth: 1 Corinthians 13:11** — *When I became a man, I put the ways of childhood behind me."* Memorize this as your mantra against immaturity.

- **Growth Vitamins:** Track your personal growth — spiritually, emotionally, financially. Celebrate progress.

- **Accountability Capsules:** Don't walk alone. Surround yourself with mature believers who can sharpen you (**Proverbs 27:17**).

- **Peace Tonic:** Release the guilt of carrying someone else's growth. Their refusal wasn't your responsibility.

HOLY SPIRIT CONSULT

Patient Note: "Lord, I felt like I grew while they stayed stuck. I carried what they refused to face. Did I do something wrong?"

Holy Spirit Response: "No, you did not fail. Growth is a choice. You chose Me; they chose themselves. You can't grow someone who refuses My hand. But I am still completing My work in you. I am still maturing you into wholeness. Do not confuse their stagnation with your progress. Walk forward — I am with you."

Scripture: **Philippians 1:6** — *He who began a good work in you will carry it on to completion."*

GUIDED PRAYER

"God, I confess I tried to carry someone who refused to grow. I felt drained, small, and frustrated. But I thank You that You are faithful to mature me.

Heal me from the wounds of immaturity. Teach me to trust Your growth process, even when people resist it. Give me peace to release what wasn t my burden and courage to keep growing in You. Amen."

✳ DECLARATIONS

1. I am growing, and I will not apologize for it.

2. Their immaturity does not define my future.

3. God is completing His good work in me.

4. I release the burden of carrying someone else's growth

5. My maturity will attract God's promises, not repel them.

▉ Journal Reflection Page

- **When did I first notice immaturity dragging down my marriage?**

_____

_____

_____

_____

_____

_____

- **How did I try to carry their growth for them?**

_____

_____

_____

_____

_____

_____

- **What lies did I believe about my role in "fixing" their maturity?**

_____

_____

_____

_____

_____

_____

- **Where has God matured me through this painful season?**

_____

_____

_____

_____

_____

- **What practical steps can I take to keep growing in Christ today?**

_____

_____

_____

"Some couples don't grow apart—they just get tired of babysitting someone who refuses to grow. Maturity is a choice, not a wedding gift."

-DR. PATRICIA S. TANNER

Chapter 8

Your Momma Shouldn't Have Been The Third Wheel

📑 SYMPTOM

🩺 WHEN MARRIAGE BECOMES A FAMILY REUNION THAT YOU DIDN'T SIGN UP FOR

Here s the truth no one wants to say out loud: some marriages don't fail because of money, infidelity, or even abuse. They fail because one or both spouses never cut the cord. You didn't just marry your spouse — you married their mother, their father, their siblings, and sometimes their whole opinionated extended family. And in case you missed the memo, covenant was designed for *two,* not for a family reunion.

The symptoms look like this:

- Every argument has a new referee — and it's their momma.

- You find out about decisions *after* they've been discussed at the family dinner table.

- Your spouse quotes their parents 'advice more than God's Word.

- Boundaries? Nonexistent. Mom has a key to your house, dad has opinions about your finances, and your marriage bed feels crowded — not physically, but spiritually.

Sarcastic reality check: if you wanted to be in a polygamous relationship, you would've signed up for TLC's *Sister Wives.* Instead, you married one person and got a whole committee. And let's be clear: this isn't about hating families. It's about misplaced priorities. When marriage feels like a triangle with your spouse and their mother, resentment isn't far behind.

And you felt it in your spirit long before the fights started in the flesh. God designed marriage for *leaving and cleaving* (**Genesis 2:24**). When that didn't happen, your spirit flagged it as "danger." But culture, guilt, or family tradition told you to stay quiet. And year after year, you shrank, while your spouse's loyalty stayed chained to their parents.

The real symptom? You weren't fighting just for attention — you were fighting for covenant. And nothing exhausts a marriage faster than competing with someone who should've stayed in their own lane.

When you said, "*I do,*" you thought you were marrying one person. But somewhere along the way, you realized you accidentally married an entire family. Suddenly, your living room feels like a revolving door for in-laws. Decisions about your own household seem to require votes from siblings, cousins, or even a parent who can't seem to let go. It feels less like a covenant between two people and more like you unknowingly signed a contract with a family reunion committee.

This symptom is one of the most exhausting silent killers of marriage. It's not always malicious — sometimes it's cultural, sometimes it's tradition, and sometimes it's just plain unhealthy attachment. But no matter the reason, when outside voices are louder than the covenant vows inside your home, the marriage begins to lose its center. The husband feels undermined when his mother's opinion always trumps his decisions. The wife feels disrespected when her family knows more about their problems than her husband does. What should be sacred and private becomes public and polluted.

And it doesn't stop at opinions. When families fail to respect boundaries, they can stir division without even realizing it. A mother-in-law criticizes how the kids are raised. A sibling whispers about how "you could do better." A cousin has a spare key and treats your home like their second apartment. While these things might look like "closeness" on the surface, underneath they are termites gnawing away at trust and unity.

The Bible speaks to this very issue. **Genesis 2:24** sets the foundation: *"That is why a man leaves his father and mother and is united to his wife, and they become one flesh."* The word "leave" is not about abandoning honor or respect — it's about setting new boundaries. Marriage is not just about joining together, but also about creating distance from the family dynamic you came from. Not separation in love, but separation in authority. Because until there is a clear leaving, there cannot be a true cleaving.

When marriage becomes a family reunion, conflict is inevitable. Loyalty gets tested. A spouse starts to feel like they're in competition with a mother, a father, or even siblings. Conversations that should stay between two people become town hall meetings with too many advisors. The sacredness of the covenant is slowly eroded by the noise of other voices. And instead of building a home, the couple ends up maintaining a campground where everybody else gets to pitch a tent.

This symptom leaves many marriages gasping for air, because privacy is oxygen to a covenant. When too many people have access to the inner chambers of a relationship, trust suffocates. And until boundaries are established, the marriage will always feel hijacked by people who were never supposed to sit in the driver's seat.

God s Blueprint For Boundaries And Covenant

Let s anchor this in truth: marriage is a covenant between two people and God — not two people, God, and their extended relatives. **Genesis 2:24** sets the standard: Leaving comes *before* cleaving. You can't cling to your parents while claiming to cling to your spouse.

When spouses fail to "leave," marriages fail to thrive. In-laws become outlaws when boundaries are absent. And let's get sarcastic for a second: nothing says "romantic" like your spouse's mother weighing in on your sex life, parenting choices, and kitchen cleaning schedule. If the Holy Spirit isn't running the house, but their mom is, covenant has already been hijacked.

Jesus Himself affirmed boundaries. In **Luke 14:26**, He said, *If anyone comes to me and does not hate father and mother, wife and children, brothers and sisters—yes, even their own life—such a person cannot be my disciple."* He wasn't telling us to despise family, but to prioritize rightly. God first, spouse second. Parents, siblings, and extended family come after. Anything else is disorder — and disorder breeds destruction.

Control from in-laws is just another form of misplaced authority. **Exodus 20:12** tells us to honor our father and mother — but honor doesn't mean obeying them into adulthood. Honor means respect, not bondage. Marriage creates a *new* family unit. That means loyalty shifts. And when that doesn't happen, you're not living in covenant, you're living in divided allegiance.

Here s the teaching boiled down:

- **Marriage requires leaving before cleaving.** Without boundaries, in-laws become third wheels.

- **Loyalty must be reordered.** God first, spouse second, everyone else after.

- **Boundaries are biblical.** Even Jesus modeled separation to fulfill His calling.

- **Divorce often exposes misplaced priorities.** Papers reveal what the Spirit already grieved: divided loyalty broke covenant.

Sarcastic truth? You didn't fail because you wanted boundaries. You failed because they didn't want to grow a spine. God didn't call you to be married to a mama's boy or daddy's princess forever. He called you to be one flesh. And one flesh doesn't need a parental referee.

But here s the hope: even if family interference suffocated your marriage, God can restore order in your spirit. **Psalm 68:6** says, *God sets the lonely in families."* Divorce may have removed you from a toxic family dynamic, but God Himself places you in His family, where boundaries are respected and covenant is honored.

God s design for marriage is crystal clear: it is a covenant between two people and Him — not two people and their extended family. That doesn't mean we dishonor parents or neglect family ties. In fact, **Ephesians 6:2–3** reminds us to *Honor your father and mother"* as the first commandment with a promise. But honor is not the same as control. Honor respects. Control dictates. And God never intended for your parents, siblings, or relatives to be the third strand in your cord of covenant.

 Boundaries are not unbiblical — they are divine. God Himself modeled boundaries in creation. He separated light from darkness, water from land, and set borders around nations. Boundaries preserve order, and in marriage, boundaries

preserve unity. Without them, confusion reigns. With them, peace flourishes.

A godly boundary in marriage says: *We decide together.* It says: *We keep certain matters private.* It says: *We love and respect our families, but they do not dictate our covenant.* This is not rebellion; it's responsibility. Because when God joined Adam and Eve, He didn't add their parents to the equation. He gave them to each other — naked, unashamed, and free to build a new life without interference.

Establishing boundaries also requires courage. It's not easy to say "no" to the family you love, especially when they believe they are helping. But wisdom means knowing when help is harm. **Proverbs 4:23** instructs us to *Guard your heart   above all else, for it determines the course of your life."* Guarding your marriage covenant is part of guarding your heart. And sometimes, that means locking certain doors to protect what God has entrusted to you.

God's blueprint for covenant is always centered on oneness. That's why Jesus reiterated in Matthew 19:6, *So they are no longer two, but one flesh. Therefore, what God has joined together, let no one separate.'"* No one" includes well-meaning parents. "No one" includes meddling siblings. "No one" includes anyone who believes their voice should outweigh the voice of God in your covenant.

When boundaries are honored, marriage flourishes. A husband feels empowered to lead without fear of his authority being undermined. A wife feels secure knowing her voice matters more than outside opinions. Children grow up in stability instead of divided loyalties. And above all, the couple learns to rely on God and each other instead of being tossed around by family expectations.

God is not calling marriages to isolation but to covenant protection. Families can still be celebrated, respected, and embraced. But when the covenant is compromised by outside influence, it's time to reset the boundary lines. Because God's design is not family reunion chaos — it is covenant clarity. And when a couple aligns with that blueprint, they discover that the safest, healthiest, and most God-honoring marriage is one where the home is ordered by God, not managed by the crowd.

🕊️ FAITH PRESCRIPTION

- **Daily Dose of Truth: Genesis 2:24** — *That is why a man leaves his father and mother and is united to his wife."* Meditate on the word *leave.*

- **Boundary Vitamins:** Write down where boundaries were violated. Pray for wisdom on how to establish them in the future.

- **Order Capsules:** Remember God's order: God → Spouse → Family. Anything else is dysfunction.

- **Peace Tonic:** Release resentment toward in-laws. Forgiveness restores peace, even if boundaries fail.

🕊️ HOLY SPIRIT CONSULT

Patient's Note: "Lord, I felt like I was never enough because their family always came first. Did I matter at all?"

Holy Spirit Response: "You mattered to Me. Your covenant mattered to Me. Their divided loyalty wounded you, but I see you. I designed marriage for oneness, not overcrowding. I will restore your sense of worth, and I will surround you with people who honor you without competition. You are Mine, and My family has room for you."

Scripture: Psalm 27:10 — *Though my father and mother forsake me, the Lord will receive me."*

🙏 GUIDED PRAYER

God, I confess that family interference drained my marriage. I felt small, unseen, and unchosen. But I thank You that You see me and choose me daily. Heal me from wounds of rejection. Restore my sense of worth. Teach me to establish godly boundaries without guilt. Surround me with healthy, Spirit-led relationships. Amen."

✸ DECLARATIONS

1. I am chosen and seen by God.

2. My worth is not measured by divided loyalty.

3. Boundaries are holy, not selfish.

4. I release resentment and choose peace.

5. God places me in His family, where covenant is honored.

📖 Journal Reflection Page

- **Where did I notice family interference stealing peace from my marriage?**

_____

_____

_____

- **How did divided loyalty affect my sense of worth?**

_____

_____

_____

_____

- **What lies did I believe about honoring parents vs. obeying them in adulthood?**

_____

_____

_____

_____

- **How does Genesis 2:24 reset my view of covenant?**

_____

_____

_____

_____

- **What boundaries will I commit to setting in future relationships?**

_____

_____

_____

_____

Chapter 9

The Perfect Marriage Only Existed On Instagram

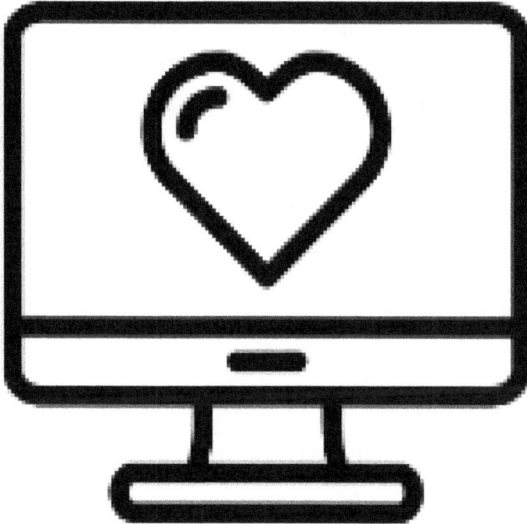

SYMPTOM

FILTERED LOVE, UNFILTERED PAIN

Instagram. Facebook. TikTok. Whatever app you scroll, you'll find couples posing in matching outfits, sipping lattes at overpriced coffee shops, or taking sunset walks on the beach.   Their captions say things like *Married to my best friend"* or *Love you forever, babe."* Meanwhile, your reality looks more like unpaid bills, an unfinished argument, and someone snoring on the couch while you scroll, wondering where it all went wrong.

The symptom here is comparison — the slow poison that kills gratitude and magnifies disappointment. Your marriage wasn't perfect, but it also wasn't as picture-perfect as the filtered feeds online. You start measuring your reality against their highlight reels, and suddenly, what used to feel normal now feels like failure.

It starts small:

- "Why doesn't he buy me flowers like her husband does?"

- "Why can't she look at me like that influencer looks at her man?"

- "Why do they seem so happy while I'm barely surviving?"

But comparison grows. It shifts from noticing differences to resenting them. It fuels entitlement: *I deserve what they have."* It feeds discontent: *If my spouse really loved me, they d act like that."* And before you know it, you're more married to scrolling than to your spouse.

Sarcasm time: if Instagram marriages were reality, divorce courts would be empty. Everyone would wake up with good hair, smiling spouses, and breakfasts served on wooden trays with artisanal jam. But you know better. Behind every filtered photo is unfiltered pain. What you don't see is the fight before the family photo, the therapy sessions, the silent treatments, and the tears cried in bathrooms.

But here s the deeper layer: unrealistic expectations don't start on Instagram. They start in the spirit. You expected your spouse to fill needs only God can meet. You thought marriage would fix your loneliness, cure your insecurity, and heal your wounds. But marriage isn't the Savior. Jesus is. When expectations are misaligned, disappointment is guaranteed.

The Spirit may have nudged you early: *Don t idolize marriage. Don t idolize appearances."* But you ignored it because society — and sometimes church culture — told you that marriage was the ultimate achievement. You entered with expectations no human could meet, and when reality failed to measure up, resentment grew.

The symptom? Your marriage was never competing with Instagram couples. It was competing with the idol in your own mind. And idols always disappoint.

We live in a generation that thrives on filters. Instagram filters, Snapchat filters, TikTok edits — everything designed to polish, blur, or highlight only the good angles. But here's the problem: filters might work for photos, but they destroy marriages. Because when you're only giving your spouse filtered love, you're withholding the real you. And when the real you finally shows up, the pain is unfiltered and overwhelming.

This symptom often begins subtly. A couple posts smiling pictures on social media, hands clasped, matching outfits, with hashtag

#Blessed in the caption — but behind closed doors, conversations are tense, affection is cold, and resentment is building. The public sees the "filtered" version of love, but the private reality is a slow bleed of neglect, bitterness, and unspoken frustration. What started as trying to "save face" becomes a double life. One image for the world, another truth for the home.

The danger is that filtered love always leads to unfiltered pain. Why? Because you can't sustain a marriage on appearances. You can only fake love for so long before exhaustion and disillusionment set in. The spouse who feels unseen eventually starts wondering, *Am I only good enough for the highlight reel but not worthy of real affection?* The partner who hides behind filters eventually feels trapped, living a lie that suffocates authenticity.

Scripture warns us about this kind of duplicity. Jesus said in **Matthew 23:27**, *"Woe to you… you are like whitewashed tombs, which look beautiful on the outside but on the inside are full of dead men's bones and everything unclean."* It's a harsh truth, but the same principle applies to marriages that prioritize appearance over authenticity. They look beautiful on the outside but rot internally from neglect, pride, or unaddressed wounds.

Filtered love is also rooted in comparison. The couple isn't just hiding their flaws — they're often trying to compete with other couples. The endless scroll of "perfect" vacations, anniversaries, and proposals on social media becomes the silent third wheel in their covenant. What should be a marriage built on trust becomes a competition for likes, comments, and validation. And when comparison is the compass, insecurity will always be the destination.

This symptom leaves people deeply wounded, because pain that is hidden eventually explodes. Couples who live in filtered love spend more time managing their image than mending their relationship. By the time the mask slips, the unfiltered pain is raw and brutal — infidelity, resentment, emotional neglect, or divorce papers signed in silence. The highlight reel becomes a horror story nobody saw coming, and the couple who "looked perfect" is now another cautionary tale.

God s Standard Is Covenant, Not Comparison

Let s dismantle this lie: marriage was never meant to look perfect. It was meant to look holy. **Ephesians 5:25–27** says, *Husbands, love your wives, just as Christ loved the church and gave himself up for her to make her holy, cleansing her by the washing with water through the word, and to present her to himself as a radiant church."* Notice: the goal isn't perfection — it's holiness.

Social media thrives on illusion. It sells the fantasy that happiness is measured by likes, trips, gifts, and curated posts. But God measures marriage by sacrifice, service, and love in action. Instagram shows #CoupleGoals; God shows covenant that endures storms.

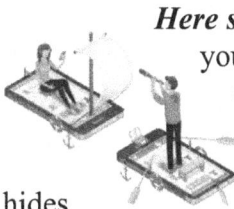

Here s the sarcastic truth: you can filter a photo, but you can't filter a covenant. The Spirit sees beyond captions into hearts. He knows if you're posting Bible verses together but fighting like enemies in private. He knows if your anniversary photo hides a decade of resentment. He knows when you're living for likes instead of living for love.

Comparison isn't new. Long before Instagram, people looked at others and envied. **James 3:16** warns, *For where you have envy and selfish ambition, there you find disorder and every evil practice."* Envy opens the door to destruction — not just in marriages, but in souls.

Here s another layer: comparison thrives when intimacy with God dies. When you stop seeking His affirmation, you crave human applause. When you stop believing His promises, you measure yourself against other people's highlight reels. And when that happens in marriage, divorce is never far behind. Because no spouse can compete with fantasy.

But God's standard is different. He calls us to contentment. **Philippians 4:11–12** says, *I have learned to be content whatever the circumstances. I know what it is to be in need, and I know what it is to have plenty. I have learned the secret of being content in any and every situation."* Contentment doesn't come from matching someone else's marriage — it comes from trusting God in your own.

Here s the teaching boiled down:

- **Comparison kills covenant.** You can't love your spouse if you're resenting them for not being someone else.

- **Perfection is an illusion.** Every marriage has struggles, no matter how shiny the feed looks.

- **God calls for holiness, not hashtags.** Marriage is about reflecting Christ, not collecting likes.

- **Divorce often reveals the idols.** Sometimes the end of a marriage exposes what we worship: perfection, appearances, or fantasy.

But here s the hope: God doesn't leave you in the ruins of comparison. He invites you back into truth. He says, *You don t need to compete. You don t need to compare. You are loved, chosen, and enough."*

God never called marriage to be a photo-op; He called it to be a covenant. His design was not about outshining another couple or pretending to have it all together, but about two people becoming one in honesty, sacrifice, and love. Covenant love doesn't hide flaws; it embraces them with grace. Covenant love doesn't compete with others; it commits to growth together. Covenant love doesn't rely on filters; it thrives in authenticity.

In **1 Corinthians 13:4–7**, Paul lays out God's standard for love: *Love is patient, love is kind. It does not envy, it does not boast, it is not proud. It does not dishonor others, it is not self-seeking, it is not easily angered, it keeps no record of wrongs. Love does not delight in evil but rejoices with the truth. It always protects, always trusts, always hopes, always perseveres."* Notice that covenant love is rooted in truth, not appearances. It rejoices in the raw, unfiltered reality of two imperfect people choosing grace daily.

Comparison is poison to covenant. **Galatians 6:4–5** reminds us, *Each one should test their own actions. Then they can take pride in themselves alone, without comparing themselves to someone else, for each one should carry their own load."*

God doesn't measure your marriage against your neighbor's. He measures it against His Word. And His Word is clear — love is not performance, it's perseverance.

God's standard calls couples to strip away the filters and step into freedom. That freedom says: *We don t have to look perfect, we just have to stay faithful.* It says: *Our marriage is not for likes or applause, it s for God s glory.* It says: *Even in our flaws, God s grace is enough to hold us together.* When you embrace covenant over comparison, you stop competing with an illusion and start cultivating intimacy with the one God gave you.

Practically, this means building rhythms of authenticity. It means confessing instead of concealing, forgiving instead of pretending, and loving in action instead of curating appearances. It means remembering that your spouse doesn't need you to be perfect — they need you to be present. It means holding fast to the covenant you made before God, knowing that His grace covers what your filters never could.

At its core, God's standard for marriage reflects His relationship with us. He never loved us with filters. **Romans 5:8** declares, *But God demonstrates his own love for us in this: While we were still sinners, Christ died for us."*

That's raw, unfiltered, sacrificial love. And that's the same love He calls husbands and wives to reflect. A love that doesn't need polishing or performance to be powerful.

Covenant is the cure for comparison. When you anchor your marriage in God's standard, the highlight reel fades, and what remains is a love that is real, resilient, and rooted in Christ. And while it may never look picture-perfect to the world, it will reflect the beauty of God's design — unfiltered love that endures.

FAITH PRESCRIPTION

- **Daily Dose of Truth: Philippians 4:11** — *I have learned to be content whatever the circumstances."* Let this anchor you against envy.

- **Reality Vitamins:** Remind yourself daily: "Instagram is a highlight reel, not the whole story."

- **Contentment Capsules:** Thank God for three things daily — not filtered, not staged, just real blessings.

- **Peace Tonic:** Limit scrolling. Instead of comparing, pray for those couples. Shift envy into intercession.

❄ HOLY SPIRIT CONSULT

Patient Note: "Lord, I felt like my marriage never measured up. I compared it to everyone else's, and I always came up short. Did I fail?"

Holy Spirit Response: "You didn't fail because you weren't perfect. You stumbled because you chased illusions instead of intimacy with Me. My standard is holiness, not perfection. My love is not filtered or staged. Walk with Me, and I will teach you contentment and peace beyond comparison."

Scripture: Hebrews 13:5 — *Keep your lives free from the love of money and be content with what you have, because God has said, Never will I leave you; never will I forsake you.'"*

🙏 GUIDED PRAYER

God, I confess that I compared my marriage, my life, and myself to others. I resented what I didn t have instead of thanking You for what I did. Forgive me for idolizing perfection and illusions.

Teach me to be content with You. Heal the wounds of disappointment and envy. Restore my peace and help me see my worth through Your eyes, not through filters. Amen."

�֍ DECLARATIONS

1. I am not defined by comparison.

2. Perfection is an illusion — I choose holiness instead.

3. Contentment in Christ is my anchor.

4. My worth is not measured by likes, gifts, or filtered photos.

5. God is enough, and His presence makes me enough.

📓 Journal Reflection Page

• **When did I first begin comparing my marriage to others?**

_____

_____

_____

_____

• **How did comparison affect my contentment and peace?**

_____

_____

_____

_____

• **What lies did I believe about perfection and worth?**

_____

_____

_____

_____

- How does Philippians 4:11 reshape my view of contentment?

_____

_____

_____

_____

_____

_____

- What practical steps can I take to silence comparison in my daily life?

_____

_____

_____

_____

_____

_____

_____

_____

_____

_____

_____

"Don't let a filtered post fool you—God deals in truth, not illusions. A picture-perfect marriage online can be a storm sheltering behind a smiling selfie."

-DR. PATRICIA S. TANNER

Chapter 10

Abuse Wasn't God's Idea Of Marriage

📋 SYMPTOM

🩺 WHEN SUBMISSION FEELS LIKE SLAVERY

Let's be brutally honest. One of the most misquoted, misused, and manipulated scriptures in marriage is **Ephesians 5:22** — *Wives, submit yourselves to your own husbands as you do to the Lord."* Abusers love this verse. Control freaks weaponize it. Churches sometimes teach it wrong. And too many women (and men too) have been crushed under its misapplication.

Here s the symptom: you stayed in something God never called holy because someone told you leaving would mean rebellion. Submission became a prison, not a partnership. You were told to "honor God" by enduring bruises, emotional manipulation, and constant belittling. You were told God would bless you if you just kept quiet, kept praying, and kept taking it.

Sarcasm check: if God's design for marriage was one spouse living in fear while the other plays Pharaoh, then congratulations — the Exodus was pointless. But the Bible you hold doesn't describe submission as slavery. It describes it as mutual love, service, and sacrifice.

Let s call it for what it is: abuse. Abuse in words. Abuse in silence. Abuse in control. Abuse in physical violence. Abuse in manipulation leaves you questioning your sanity. Abuse wrapped in Christian language is still abuse. Just because someone quotes scripture doesn't mean they're living it. Satan himself quoted scripture to Jesus in the wilderness (**Matthew 4**). If the devil can twist God's Word, abusers can too.

The symptom? Many marriages ended — not because someone failed to submit, but because submission was distorted into domination. And when domination replaces devotion, covenant is already broken.

Few words in marriage trigger more heated debates than "submission." For some, it's a word that feels heavy, outdated, and even dangerous. Too often, it has been twisted, misapplied, or weaponized — leaving one spouse feeling silenced, diminished, or trapped. Instead of becoming a pathway to unity, the call for submission becomes a power struggle where one person rules and the other merely exists.

This symptom shows up when "submission" gets confused with domination. The husband interprets his role as dictator instead of servant leader, while the wife feels reduced to a servant instead of a partner. What God designed to be mutual honor turns into a dynamic where one voice is amplified and the other is silenced. When this happens, marriage no longer reflects the beautiful dance of grace and respect but starts resembling a prison of control.

Submission that feels like slavery strips marriage of its God-given equality. In **Genesis 2:18**, God said, *It is not good for the man to be alone. I will make a helper suitable for him."* The word "helper" in Hebrew (ezer) does not mean "assistant" or "less than." It's the same word used for God Himself when He helps His people (**Psalm 33:20**). That means wives were never designed to be doormats — they were designed to stand shoulder to shoulder with their husbands as powerful, equal image-bearers of God. When marriages twist submission into control, they distort God's original blueprint.

The symptoms are especially painful because it cloaks itself in scripture. Passages like **Ephesians 5:22** (*Wives, submit yourselves to your own husbands as you do to the Lord"*) are often quoted, but rarely are the verses that follow emphasized. Because the truth is, if submission is demanded rather than nurtured through love, it ceases to be biblical submission and becomes manipulation. And manipulation is not God's plan for any marriage.

When submission feels like slavery, love becomes suffocating instead of liberating. Resentment builds, intimacy dies, and one or both partners carry wounds that God never intended. Marriage, which should be the safest place on earth, becomes a battlefield of dominance and survival.

God Calls For Sacrifice, Not Subjugation

Let's clean this up with scripture. **Ephesians 5:25** says, *Husbands, love your wives, just as Christ loved the church and gave himself up for her."* You know what that means? True headship doesn't look like control — it looks like crucifixion. Jesus didn't abuse the church into obedience; He died for her. He didn't demand loyalty through fear; He won her through love.

If submission is about one spouse silencing their voice and erasing their worth, that's not biblical submission. That's bondage. And **Galatians 5:1** declares, *It is for freedom that Christ has set us free. Stand firm, then, and do not let yourselves be burdened again by a yoke of slavery."* God never designed marriage to be a yoke of slavery.

Here s where the sarcasm kicks in again: if "submission" means never questioning, never disagreeing, never having a voice, then apparently God wasted His time giving women wisdom, discernment, and the Holy Spirit. Spoiler alert: He didn't. The Spirit dwells in both husband and wife, which means both voices matter.

Abuse is not submission. Abuse is sin. Abuse mocks covenant. Abuse contradicts love. Abuse violates the very image of God in a spouse. And to endure abuse under the banner of "holiness" is not faith — it's deception.

Now let s be clear: not every marriage argument or imperfection equals abuse. But when someone repeatedly breaks your body, spirit, or sense of safety, that's not just "struggle" — that's violence. And God does not bless violence disguised as authority. **Malachi 2:16 (NIV)** says, *The man who hates and divorces his wife," says the Lord, the God of Israel, does violence to the one he should protect."* God literally calls abusive betrayal **violence** — and He hates it.

Here s the teaching boiled down:

- **Submission ≠ Slavery.** It's about honor and partnership, not erasure.

- **Headship = Sacrifice.** Christ modeled leadership through dying, not dominating.

- **Abuse cancels covenant.** Violence isn't just a sin, it's covenant-breaking.

- **God is protective, not passive.** He doesn't tell you to endure abuse "for His glory." He calls you to freedom, healing, and wholeness.

This is why many divorces happen — not because people abandoned God's design, but because abuse corrupted it. And walking away from abuse is not walking away from God. It's walking toward Him.

God's blueprint for marriage was never about one person overpowering the other. It was always about both reflecting Christ's love through mutual honor, respect, and sacrifice. In fact, before Paul ever talks about wives submitting to husbands in **Ephesians 5**, he begins with verse 21: *Submit to one another out of reverence for Christ."* Mutual

submission is the foundation — a rhythm where both husband and wife lay down pride for the sake of unity.

Husbands are not called to be tyrants; they are called to be living reflections of Christ's sacrificial love. Verse 25 makes it clear: *Husbands, love your wives, just as Christ loved the church and gave himself up for her."* Christ's leadership looked like washing feet (**John 13**), carrying a cross, and laying down His life. If leadership in marriage doesn't resemble that kind of humility and sacrifice, it's not biblical leadership at all — it's selfishness disguised as authority.

True submission in God's design isn't about silence or oppression. It's about trust, love, and partnership under the lordship of Christ. Submission means yielding to one another in love, not stripping away a person's voice or worth. It's about aligning hearts toward God together. It's not slavery — it's synergy.

God's standard calls us higher than cultural caricatures of "submission." It calls for a love that empowers, not enslaves. It calls for husbands to honor their wives as co-heirs of grace (**1 Peter 3:7**), recognizing that both are equally valuable in God's kingdom. It calls for wives to walk confidently in their identity as daughters of the King, knowing their worth is not diminished by loving partnership but strengthened through covenant.

At its heart, submission and sacrifice are two sides of the same coin. Both husband and wife are invited into the same calling: *lay down your life so that love can live.* When that happens, submission is no longer a weapon — it's worship. It's not forced obedience, but freely chosen alignment, motivated by love, anchored in Christ, and empowered by the Spirit.

This is why God calls for sacrifice, not subjugation. Sacrifice says, *I lay down my rights for your good.* Subjugation says, *You don t have rights at all.* Sacrifice builds intimacy. Subjugation builds fear. And God's design has always been love that casts out fear (**1 John 4:18**).

When marriages embrace this truth, the word "submission" is redeemed. It no longer feels like slavery but like the beautiful exchange of love that mirrors Christ and His Church — not oppressive but liberating; not silencing, but empowering; not demeaning, but divine.

💊 FAITH PRESCRIPTION

- **Scripture Syrup:** Galatians 5:1 — *It is for freedom that Christ has set us free.''* Repeat this daily until it silences the lie that abuse is "holy suffering."

- **Reality Capsules:** Write down the difference between submission and slavery. Tear up the lies that told you to stay silent.

- **Healing Ointment:** Journal the moments God gave you strength to resist abuse — that wasn't rebellion, it was revelation.

- **Covenant Vitamins:** Remember: God hates violence. If He hates it, He never asked you to endure it.

🕊 HOLY SPIRIT CONSULT

Patient Note:" Lord, I thought leaving was failure. They told me I wasn't 'submissive enough. 'They told me I dishonored You by walking away."

Holy Spirit Response:" You did not fail Me. You refused to bow to bondage. Submission to Me is freedom, not slavery. I never asked you to worship abuse. I asked you to walk in truth. I am not ashamed of you — I am proud that you chose life."

Scripture: Psalm 34:18 — *The Lord is close to the brokenhearted and saves those who are crushed in spirit."*

🙏 GUIDED PRAYER

"Father, I release the lie that submission equals silence. I release the shame of leaving abuse behind. I choose to believe that You never designed covenant to be violent, manipulative, or cruel. Heal the places in me where fear and control left scars. Teach me to hear Your voice above the noise of culture and abuse. Thank You that You are not a God who endorses harm but a God who rescues. In Jesus 'name, Amen."

✴ DECLARATIONS

1. Abuse is not submission, and submission is not slavery.

2. My worth is not erased by leaving bondage.

3. God loves me enough to protect me from harm.

4. I am not a failure for walking in freedom.

5. Christ died for me to live free, not bruised.

📔 Journal Reflection Page

- **How was "submission" misused against me?**

_____

_____

_____

_____

_____

- **What scriptures were twisted to silence me, and what truth corrects them?**

_____

_____

_____

_____

_____

- **How do I feel knowing God hates violence done against me?**

_____

_____

_____

_____

_____

- **What does Christ's model of sacrificial love teach me about real covenant?**

_____

_____

_____

_____

_____

- **What step can I take today to reclaim freedom without guilt?**

_____

_____

_____

_____

_____

_____

_____

_____

_____

_____

_____

_____

_____

Chapter 11

Spiritually Unequally Yoked- One Went To Bible Study, The Other Went To The Club

(Faith Differences)

SYMPTOM

WHEN BELIEFE BECOMES BATTLEFIELD-WHY FAITH GAPS CREATE FRACTURES

Here's the thing nobody tells you when you're lovestruck and quoting "love is patient, love is kind" at your wedding: patience and kindness can't fix a spiritual chasm. When you're unequally yoked, what feels like "cute differences" in year one becomes open warfare by year ten.

At first, you thought, *It s fine, opposites attract."* You figured his "not into church" vibe was just a phase. You assumed her "Jesus is optional" stance would melt once she saw your devotion. Spoiler alert: it didn't.

Fast forward, and you're arguing about whether to tithe or buy another flat screen. You're praying over your kids at night while your spouse is blasting music that makes demons feel at home. You're begging for church on Sunday while they're nursing a hangover from Saturday. Welcome to the battleground of faith gaps — where belief collides with disbelief and your marriage is the casualty.

The symptom is this: spiritual misalignment doesn't stay cute. It grows teeth. You start resenting each other for choices rooted in two different value systems. For you, God is the center. For them, God is an accessory. And no matter how much you "compromise," the cracks spread because your foundation is speaking two different languages.

Sunday Mornings vs. Saturday Nights
Opposite Lifestyles Under One Roof

Picture this: You're ironing church clothes for yourself and the kids, praying for strength, while your spouse is ironing their outfit for the club. Same house, two different destinations. That tension doesn't just live in the closet — it spills into every conversation.

You want to raise your children in the fear of the Lord. They say, "Don't be so strict, let them find their own truth." You believe in saving intimacy for marriage. They roll their eyes and say, "We're human." You want to build your budget around stewardship and tithing. They want to blow money on bottles, parties, or "self-care" that looks suspiciously like selfishness.

Let s get sarcastically real: you're basically living with a roommate who happens to share your last name but not your faith. And you can't Netflix-and-chill your way out of that.

This is why Paul warned us in **2 Corinthians 6:14** — *Do not be unequally yoked with unbelievers. For what partnership has righteousness with lawlessness? Or what fellowship has light with darkness?"* The Bible isn't being dramatic — it's being practical. If two oxen are yoked together but pulling in different directions, they don't plow straight. The cart flips. The harvest is ruined. Sound familiar?

The teaching here is simple: faith isn't just personal preference; it's the compass that directs everything. Two compasses pointing in opposite directions can't lead a marriage forward. They'll pull until the yoke snaps — and when it does, it hurts.

Marriage was meant to be a sanctuary, but when two people don't share the same spiritual foundation, it often feels more like a battlefield. What God designed for unity and peace becomes a place of constant conflict because the deepest part of who you are — your faith — is constantly colliding with the deepest part of who your spouse is. Faith isn't just a side note in life; it informs your values, your choices, your priorities, and your vision for the future. When one person builds their life on Christ and the other builds on something else, the cracks begin to show.

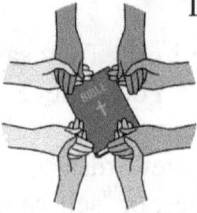

This symptom surfaces in daily life. The believer wants to pray over the kids before school, but the other spouse rolls their eyes. One wants to tithe faithfully, but the other sees it as "throwing money away." One spends Sunday mornings in worship, the other spends it recovering from Saturday night. What started as "opposites attract" quickly turns into "opposites attack," because two visions are pulling in two different directions. And as **Amos 3:3** reminds us, *"Do two walk together unless they have agreed to do so?"*

The battlefield isn't always loud. Sometimes it's silent — the tension of sitting next to someone who doesn't share the most important part of your soul. Sometimes it's loneliness inside a marriage, watching your spouse dismiss or even mock the very faith that carries you through life. And that loneliness cuts deeper than any argument ever could, because it is a loneliness in the spirit — a divide in the very core of your being.

Over time, faith gaps create fractures. The believer begins to feel torn between pleasing God and pleasing their spouse. Compromise starts to feel less like sacrifice and more like surrendering your convictions. The unbelieving spouse may feel judged, nagged, or pressured, which only widens the gap further. What should be a covenant of unity becomes a tug-of-war of values. And the heartbreaking truth is this: when faith becomes a battlefield, love often becomes collateral damage.

God s Blueprint On Being Yoked —
Why Spiritual Alignment Matters

Here s the bigger truth: God designed marriage as a covenant, not a contract. A covenant requires agreement at the deepest level — and nothing runs deeper than the spirit. You can agree on movies, on favorite foods, even on how many kids to have. But if you can't agree on who God is, how He leads, and what obedience looks like, then you're living in constant conflict.

Amos 3:3 is not poetic fluff — it's a survival strategy. If your spouse doesn't believe prayer changes things, your prayers for your marriage will feel like dragging a corpse uphill. If your spouse thinks church is optional, you'll spend years carrying your kids to church by yourself. If your spouse mocks your faith, you'll start questioning whether it's worth fighting for.

And here s the kicker: sometimes it wasn't even that your spouse hated God. Sometimes it was that you married them hoping they'd change — and they didn't. You signed up for a lifetime of missionary dating, confusing "potential" for "partner." And potential doesn't keep a covenant.

God's blueprint was never for you to settle for spiritual tug-of-war. His design is partnership where both hearts are surrendered to Him. Anything else is settling for chaos dressed in romance.

God never designed marriage to be a place of division. He intended it to be a union of hearts, minds, and spirits aligned toward Him. That's why Paul warns in **2 Corinthians 6:14**, *Do not be yoked together with unbelievers. For what do righteousness and wickedness have in common? Or what fellowship can light have with darkness?"*

The imagery of being "yoked" points to farming: two oxen tied together under the same wooden beam. If one ox is stronger or headed in a different direction, the entire field is plowed crooked. The harvest is compromised, not because the oxen weren't strong, but because they weren't aligned.

In marriage, being unequally yoked means the two people are pulling in different directions spiritually. One is trying to chase God's will; the other is chasing their own. One is sowing seeds of faith; the other is sowing seeds of self. It's not about superiority — it's about direction. And when the directions don't match, the journey becomes unbearable.

God s blueprint for marriage is clear: He wants a covenant that reflects His relationship with His people. That means unity, not just physically or emotionally, but spiritually. **Malachi 2:15** reminds us that God makes husband and wife "one in flesh and spirit" because He is seeking "godly offspring." That doesn't just mean children — it means fruit. A spiritually aligned marriage produces the fruit of peace, faith, love, joy, and purpose. A misaligned marriage produces confusion, strife, resentment, and brokenness.

But here's the beauty of God's design-alignment doesn't mean perfection. It means agreement. It means both spouses are committed to putting Christ at the center and walking toward Him together, even when they stumble. It means choosing prayer over pride, worship over war, grace over grudges. Spiritual alignment is less about one spouse always getting it right and more about both spouses committing to pull in the same direction — toward Jesus.

When marriages embrace God's blueprint, faith no longer becomes a battlefield. Instead, it becomes the foundation. It becomes the anchor that holds during storms, the compass that guides decisions, and the glue that binds hearts together. And where there was once fracture, there is now favor. Where there was once division, there is now divine unity.

Because in the end, God's call to be equally yoked isn't about limiting love — it's about protecting it. It's about ensuring that love has the best chance to flourish, thrive, and reflect Christ. And when two people pull together in the same direction under God's yoke, their marriage doesn't just survive — it bears fruit that testifies of His goodness.

Faith After The Fallout — Rebuilding Identity In Christ After Division

So, what now? The divorce papers are signed. The "unequal yoke" snapped, and you're sitting in the rubble, wondering if you wasted years of your life. Here's the truth: God can rebuild you, even after a marriage that broke your spirit.

The fallout is real — shame, guilt, questions like, *Did I miss God?"* But let me remind you: **Romans 8:28** says, *And we know that in all things God works for the good of those who love Him, who have been called according to His purpose."* Even the failed marriage? Yes. Even the heartbreak? Yes. Even the lonely nights where you second-guess everything? Absolutely.

Your identity is not "divorced." Your identity is "child of God." Your worth isn't based on how long you kept a marriage together — it's based on Christ keeping you together when everything else fell apart.

Rebuilding after being unequally yoked means learning this: you don't need someone else's faith to validate yours. You don't need someone else's church attendance to strengthen your walk. You don't need a partner to define your calling. God alone is enough.

And next time? You won't ignore the red flags. You won't excuse spiritual laziness as "just different personalities." You'll remember that alignment in the Spirit is worth more than chemistry in the flesh.

When a marriage ends, especially one divided by faith differences, the fallout feels like more than just papers signed in court — it feels like an earthquake in your soul. The person you once leaned on is gone. The routines that felt safe are broken. The future you pictured together dissolves like smoke. And if faith was the battlefield that finally split the two of you apart, the aftermath can leave you asking: *Where does my faith even stand now?*

Some believers, after walking through the collapse of a spiritually divided marriage, feel guilt: "Did I fail God?" Others feel shame: "What will the church think of me?" And still others feel confusion: "If God loves me, why didn't He fix this?" These questions are real, raw, and valid. The enemy loves to take advantage of these moments, whispering lies like, *You're unworthy. You're broken beyond repair. You can't be used anymore."* But the truth of God's Word says the opposite. The same God who redeems broken people is the God who redeems broken stories.

The key to faith after the fallout is not pretending the pain didn't happen but allowing Christ to rebuild your identity on His foundation instead of the wreckage of your past. **Psalm 34:18** reminds us, *The Lord is close to the brokenhearted and saves those who are crushed in spirit."* God doesn't back away from your heartbreak — He leans in closer. He doesn't define you by your divorce — He defines you by His love.

Rebuilding identity after division starts with remembering this: you are not half a person now. You are not "less than" because your marriage didn't survive. **Colossians 2:10** declares that you are *complete in Christ, who is the head over every power and* *authority.* " Complete. Whole. Entire. That means your worth never hinged on whether a spouse accepted your faith or rejected it, whether a marriage lasted or failed. Your worth has always been in Christ, and that worth never expires.

But rebuilding also means releasing. You can't walk into your new season, still chained to the bitterness of the last one. Forgiveness here isn't about saying what happened was okay — it's about refusing to let the wound become your identity. **Ephesians 4:31–32** calls us to *get rid of all bitterness, rage and anger... forgiving each other, just as in Christ God forgave you.* " Forgiveness clears the rubble so God can lay a new foundation. Without it, you're just trying to build on top of ruins.

Finally, faith after fallout means vision. The enemy wants you stuck in the rearview mirror, but God hands you a windshield. **Isaiah 43:19** says, *See, I am doing a new thing! Now it springs up; do you not perceive it?*" That "new thing" may not look like the old marriage. It may not even involve remarriage at all. But it will look like restoration — God piecing together your broken identity into something stronger, more resilient, more Christ-reflecting than before.

So yes, the division happened. Yes, the fallout was real. But your faith is not buried in the ruins. Christ specializes in resurrection stories. What others saw as an ending, God calls a beginning. And your identity isn't in the divorce, the papers, or the fallout — your identity is in the Redeemer who is building you back, brick by brick, into His image.

FAITH PRESCRIPTION

- **Scripture Syrup: 2 Corinthians 6:14** — *Do not be unequally yoked with unbelievers.* "

- **Reality Capsules:** Write down the ways spiritual misalignment showed up in your marriage. Be honest — denial keeps you stuck.

- **Healing Ointment:** Journal prayers where you thank God for pulling you out of what could have destroyed your faith completely.

- **Covenant Vitamins:** Declare daily: *"My covenant is with God first. Any future partnership must align with Him."*

🦋 HOLY SPIRIT CONSULT

Patient Note: "Lord, I feel like I failed because I couldn't keep my marriage together."

Holy Spirit Response: "Child, your worth was never tied to their worship. I saw your tears when you prayed alone. I saw your faith when they mocked you. I never left you unequally yoked — I walked beside you the entire time. Now, I am leading you into restoration, not regret."

🙏 GUIDED PRAYER

"Father, I confess I ignored Your warnings about being unequally yoked. I let my emotions lead where my spirit should have stood firm. But I thank You that Your grace covers even my mistakes.

Heal the wounds left by spiritual division. Restore my confidence in Your plan. Strengthen me to walk in alignment with Your Word and to never compromise my covenant with You again. In Jesus name, Amen."

✳ DECLARATIONS

1. My identity is not defined by divorce — it is defined by Christ.

2. God's presence fills the gap left by broken partnership.

3. Spiritual alignment is non-negotiable for my future.

4. What was fractured is being healed in God's timing.

5. I am free from shame — I am rebuilt in grace.

📖 Journal Reflection Page

- **How did being unequally yoked affect your faith and daily life?**

_____

_____

_____

_____

_____

- **What red flags did you ignore in the beginning, and why?**

_____

_____

_____

_____

_____

- How can you set boundaries in the future to ensure spiritual alignment?

_____

_____

_____

_____

_____

- Where have you seen God's hand redeeming even the fallout of divorce?

_____

_____

_____

_____

_____

_____

_____

_____

_____

_____

_____

_____

Chapter 12

From Court Papers To Clean Slates

(Healing & Redemption)

■ SYMPTOM

℘ GOD STILL WRITES REDEMPTION STORIES – DIVORCE DOESN'T DEFINE DESTINY

When the ink dries on the court papers, it feels like the period at the end of your life's sentence. Like everything you planned, prayed for, and invested in just collapsed into a pile of ashes. But here's the truth: God doesn't stop writing when lawyers start typing.

Divorce may change your marital status, but it doesn't cancel your destiny. It may end a chapter, but it doesn't delete the whole book. **Jeremiah 29:11** still stands: *For I know the plans I have for you," declares the Lord, plans to prosper you and not to harm you, plans to give you a hope and a future."* Notice it doesn't say, "Unless you get divorced." God didn't include an asterisk.

The symptom after divorce is this nagging lie: *I m damaged goods now.* "Society whispers it, family may reinforce it, and your own insecurities scream it. But redemption says otherwise. God specializes in broken stories turned beautiful. Ruth lost her husband and her homeland, but she became part of the lineage of Christ. David committed adultery and murder, yet God still called him a man after His heart. If God can redeem them, He can redeem you — court papers and all.

One of the heaviest lies people carry after divorce is this: *"My story is ruined. My destiny is done. God can't use me now."* It's the subtle whisper of shame that convinces you that your worth was tied to the success of your marriage, and because the marriage ended, so did your future. But that's not the voice of God — that's the voice of the accuser. God has never disqualified His children because of their scars. In fact, He often uses those very scars to tell the most powerful redemption stories.

Think of David. His life was a tangle of triumphs and failures, yet God still called him a man after His own heart. Think of the Samaritan woman in John 4, who had multiple broken relationships, but Jesus met her at the well and turned her story into a testimony that changed an entire town. Divorce doesn't cancel destiny — it positions you to discover that your identity was never meant to rest in a person, but in a Savior.

The symptom many divorced believers face is living like their life is permanently on pause, as if the divorce was the final chapter. But God specializes in writing "to be continued." If you woke up today, you're not disqualified. You're still chosen. You're still called. **Jeremiah 29:11** hasn't been ripped out of your Bible. God's plans are still "to prosper you and not to harm you, plans to give you hope and a future." Divorce doesn't erase destiny — it simply shifts how God will unfold it.

Forgiveness Isn't Amnesia — Choosing Healing Over Bitterness

Let s get brutally honest: forgiveness after divorce is messy. Nobody walks out of family court singing worship songs. You walk out with bruises on your ego, scars on your trust, and bitterness threatening to set up camp in your soul.

Forgiveness does *not* mean pretending it didn't happen. It doesn't mean saying, "It's fine" when it wasn't fine. It doesn't mean giving them a free pass. Forgiveness isn't amnesia — it's choosing not to let bitterness rot your heart.

Ephesians 4:31–32 lays it out: *Get rid of all bitterness, rage and anger... Be kind and compassionate to one another, forgiving each other, just as in Christ God forgave you."* Notice Paul didn't say, "Get rid of bitterness once the other person apologizes." No, forgiveness is about protecting your soul from the cancer of resentment.

Here s the sarcasm check: bitterness is like drinking poison and waiting for your ex to die. Spoiler — it won't work. You'll just end up spiritually sick while they're living their best life on Instagram. Forgiveness is your chemotherapy — it heals you, not them.

And let s be clear: forgiveness doesn't always mean reconciliation. Sometimes it means releasing them to God's hands and moving forward without the weight of hate. Because bitterness will make you yoke yourself to the past while God is trying to pull you into the future.

Forgiveness after divorce isn't about pretending you were never hurt. It isn't about erasing the memory or denying the betrayal, abandonment, or rejection you faced. Forgiveness isn't spiritual amnesia. Instead, it's the courageous choice to refuse to let bitterness become your permanent roommate. **Hebrews 12:15** warns us: *See to it that no bitter root grows up to cause trouble and defile many."* Bitterness doesn't just poison you — it seeps into every relationship, every prayer, every part of your soul.

When you forgive, you're not saying the other person was right. You're saying, *I refuse to let what they did control me any longer."* You release not because they deserve it, but because you deserve peace. Forgiveness is an act of warfare — it breaks the cycle of pain and hands your heart back to God. Jesus made this clear in **Matthew 6:14–15**: if we forgive others, our Father forgives us. Forgiveness is not just for the offender — it's for the freedom of the one offended.

The truth is you will remember. There will be triggers — old songs, old places, old texts that pop up in your mind. But healing doesn't come from erasure; it comes from surrender. Every memory can become a moment of testimony instead of torment if you let God hold it. Forgiveness transforms wounds into wisdom, scars into strength, and memories into markers of God's grace.

Purpose After Papers — God Still Uses Broken Vessels

Divorce makes you feel disqualified. Like somehow your usefulness in the Kingdom has expired because your marriage expired. But let's rip that lie apart: God has always used broken vessels.

Moses was a murderer with anger issues — yet he led a nation out of slavery. Rahab was a prostitute — yet she became a key figure in God's plan of salvation. Peter denied Jesus three times — yet he preached the first sermon that launched the church.

Your divorce does not put you on the bench of Kingdom usefulness. In fact, your brokenness might be your greatest qualification. **2 Corinthians 4:7** says, *But we have this treasure in jars of clay to show that this all-surpassing power is from God and not from us."* Your cracks don't disqualify you; they let His glory shine through.

Purpose after papers looks like this: you get to tell your story without shame. You get to help others avoid your mistakes. You get to walk with authority because you've been through the fire and didn't burn to ashes. People don't need perfect testimonies — they need real ones. And your "papers" might be the very thing God uses to set someone else free.

The gavel drops, the papers are signed, and suddenly your life feels stamped "finalized." But heaven doesn't measure your worth by legal documents. God has always specialized in using broken vessels to pour out His glory.

Second Corinthians 4:7 reminds us that we carry this treasure — the light of Christ — in jars of clay, "to show that this all-surpassing power is from God and not from us." The cracks in your story don't disqualify you — they're what allow His light to shine through.

Purpose doesn't end with papers. In fact, sometimes divorce propels you into purpose because it strips away every false identity you clung to. You learn quickly that ministry isn't about appearances; it's about availability. Look at Peter. He denied Jesus three times, yet God used him to launch the church. Look at Paul. He carried a past of persecution, but God used him to write much of the New Testament. Your "papers" may feel like an ending, but God says, *I'm just getting started."*

Maybe you thought your role as a husband or wife was the most important calling you'd ever have. But what if God is now calling you to mentor others walking the same road you just crawled out of? What if your healing becomes the key to someone else's freedom? Purpose after papers is proof that God isn't done. The ink on the decree doesn't erase the ink on your destiny.

From Boy, Bye" To Amen" —
How Faith Reclaims Your Future

Healing means shifting your vocabulary. At first, your anthem is "Boy, bye" (or "Girl, gone"). It's survival mode, fueled by anger and sass. But eventually, faith grows louder than your clapback. You start to trade bitterness for blessing, sarcasm for surrender, and rage for resilience.

Faith lets you say, *Amen"* — not because you liked what happened, but because you trust what God is doing with it. **Romans 8:28** becomes more than a verse; it becomes your survival kit: *And we know that in all things God works for the good of those who love him."*

Faith reclaims your future by refusing to let divorce write the final word. It reminds you that scars don't mean you lost — they mean you survived. Faith says, *Yes, I cried, but I m still standing. Yes, it broke me, but it didn t bury me. Yes, I lost someone, but I found my Savior again."*

From "Boy, bye" to "Amen" is the journey of the healed heart. One is reactionary; the other is redemptive. One clings to pain, the other clings to purpose. One kicks the past out, the other invites God in. That's when your story becomes more than survival — it becomes a testimony.

There's something freeing about that moment when you finally say, *Boy, bye."* But faith won't let you stop there. Because "bye" may release the person, but only "amen" will release the pain. Amen means "so be it." It's a declaration that says, *God, I trust You with what happened, and I trust You with what s next."* Faith takes you from bitterness to blessing, from victimhood to victory.

Reclaiming your future starts with agreement — not with your wounds, not with your fears, but with God's Word. **Jeremiah 1:5** reminds us that God knew you and appointed you before you were born. Divorce didn't sneak up on Him.

He's not wringing His hands in confusion, trying to come up with a backup plan. He is still sovereign. **Romans 8:28** still applies: *And we know that in **all** things God works for the good of those who love Him."*

"Boy, bye" acknowledges what broke you. But "Amen" announces that it won't keep you broken. Amen is what allows you to step out of your past without dragging yesterday's baggage into tomorrow's calling.

Faith doesn't deny that the papers were signed — faith declares that God's signature on your life is greater. And when you say "Amen" to His plan, you're not just moving on — you're moving forward.

FAITH PRESCRIPTION

- **Scripture Syrup: Jeremiah 29:11** — *For I know the plans I have for you... plans to give you a hope and a future."*

- **Reality Capsules:** Write down three lies you've believed about yourself post-divorce. Cross them out and replace them with scripture.

- **Healing Ointment:** Pray specifically for the ability to forgive, even if your emotions aren't there yet.

- **Covenant Vitamins:** Declare daily: "My future is not canceled. My purpose is not void. My God is still writing."

HOLY SPIRIT CONSULT

Patient Note: "Lord, I feel like divorce made me a failure."

Holy Spirit Response:" You are not defined by what ended. You are defined by Who began a good work in you — and I will carry it to completion (**Philippians 1:6**). I do not waste pain. I redeem it."

🙏 GUIDED PRAYER

"Father, thank You that court papers don t cancel Your promises. Heal me from bitterness and help me forgive, even when my feelings resist. Restore my identity in You, not in my past.

Open my eyes to see purpose where I ve only seen pain. Teach me to say Amen to Your plan, even when it looks different than mine. In Jesus name, Amen."

✳ DECLARATIONS

1. Divorce does not define me — destiny does.

2. I forgive so I can live healed, not bitter.

3. God's power shines through my broken places.

4. My future is still full of purpose and promise.

5. From "Boy, bye" to "Amen," I choose faith over fear.

📘 Journal Reflection Page

- **How has divorce tried to redefine your identity?**

_____

_____

_____

_____

_____

- **What areas of your heart still need forgiveness?**

_____

_____

_____

_____

- **Where have you seen God's redemption in your story already?**

_____

_____

_____

_____

_____

- **How can your testimony help someone else in their healing?**

_____

_____

_____

_____

_____

- **What does "From Boy, Bye to Amen" look like for you right now?**

_____

_____

Epilogue

Boy Bye Wasn't The End – It Was The Beginning

~ Faith Clinic Discharge Plan ~

What You Thought Was An Ending Was Actually A Rescue Mission

The day you signed those court papers, it felt like the coffin lid closed on everything you prayed for. You thought God had abandoned you, or worse — that He had punished you. But what if the ending was actually the rescue?

Sometimes God lets what we built crumble because it wasn't strong enough to hold the weight of His glory. Sometimes He allows the exit of a person who was subtracting instead of multiplying. And sometimes, divorce is not God's punishment, but His intervention.

Psalm 34:18 says, *The Lord is close to the brokenhearted and saves those who are crushed in spirit."* That word *saves* doesn't just mean rescue from sin — it means rescue from situations that were destroying us. Your ending was His rescue mission. You didn't get abandoned — you got delivered.

Faith After Failure — God s Grace Is Bigger Than Your Marriage Collapse

Let s call it what it is: divorce feels like failure. Even if you didn't cause it, even if you tried everything to save it, even if the circumstances were out of your control — your heart whispers, *I failed."*

But grace answers back louder: *You are forgiven. You are loved. You are still mine."*

Romans 8:1 declares, *There is therefore now no condemnation for those who are in Christ Jesus."* Condemnation says, "Your marriage collapsed, so you're worthless." Grace says, "Yes, your marriage collapsed, but My plan for you hasn't."

Faith after failure means you stop treating yourself like a failed exam. You are not your mistakes. You are not your heartbreak. You are not the papers stamped by the county clerk. You are a child of God, still carrying purpose, still anointed, still called. Divorce didn't cancel your assignment — it just rerouted the path.

Hope For The Next Chapter —
The Future Isn t Canceled

Divorce tricks you into believing that the future is a blank wall, nothing left to dream for, nothing left to look forward to. But hope whispers otherwise.

Isaiah 43:19 says, *See, I am doing a new thing! Now it springs up; do you not perceive it? "* God isn't out of new beginnings. He's the Author who doesn't run out of ink. The same God who parted the Red Sea, restored Job's life double, and resurrected Jesus isn't scratching His head about your situation. He's already writing your next chapter.

Your story isn't canceled; it's being rewritten. And this next part isn't just survival — it's revival. It's you laughing again, dreaming again, loving again, serving again, and realizing that the best days are not behind you. They're ahead of you.

Invitation To Heal —
Choosing Wholeness With God s Help

Divorce left scars. And scars don't disappear overnight. But here's the question: will you keep picking at the wound, or will you let God heal it?

Healing requires permission. God won't bulldoze His way into your heart — He waits for your invitation. **Revelation 3:20** says, *Here I am! I stand at the door and knock. If anyone hears my voice and* opens the door, I will come in." Healing begins when you open the door and say, *God, I can t fix this — but I know You can."*

Wholeness doesn't mean pretending it never happened. It means standing in the mirror, scars and all, and saying, *I am still here. I am still chosen. I am still whole in Him."*

Healing means you don't let bitterness own your story, shame narrate your future, or grief stop your growth. You choose God's wholeness — again and again — until His peace outweighs your pain.

🔵 FAITH PRESCRIPTION (Final Dose)

- **Scripture Syrup: Romans 8:28** — *And we know that in all things God works for the good of those who love him."*

- **Reality Capsules:** Divorce was a chapter, not the whole book. Don't confuse a plot twist with the conclusion.

- **Healing Ointment:** Stop calling yourself broken — start declaring yourself becoming.

- **Covenant Vitamins:** Daily prayer: *Lord, help me to live healed, not haunted."*

🕊 HOLY SPIRIT CONSULT

Patient Note: "God, I don't know who I am after this divorce."

Holy Spirit Response: "You are Mine. Before the papers. After the papers. Forever. I do not define you by who left you — I define you by the One who saved you."

🙏 GUIDED PRAYER

"Father, thank You for turning my ending into a beginning. Thank You for rescuing me when I thought I was ruined. Teach me to live free from condemnation, to forgive quickly, and to dream again boldly.

I surrender the pain, the past, and the pieces of my heart to You. Rewrite my story with Your grace and help me to embrace hope, healing, and wholeness in Christ. Amen."

✸ DECLARATIONS

1. Divorce was not my definition — redemption is.

2. What ended was not my destiny — God's plan continues.

3. I am healed, forgiven, and still chosen.

4. My story is still being written, and my best chapters are ahead.

5. From pain to purpose, from "Boy, bye" to "Amen" — I choose healing.

📔 Journal Reflection Page

- What false identity did divorce try to label you with?

_____

_____

_____

_____

_____

- How can you begin seeing your divorce as God's rescue, not your ruin?

_____

_____

_____

_____

- Where do you still need to forgive yourself or your ex?

_____

_____

_____

- What new chapter is God inviting you into right now?

_____

_____

_____

- Write a prayer inviting God to finish rewriting your story with healing and wholeness.

_____

_____

_____

_____

Divorce Edition .

From **Chapter 1's wounds** to **Chapter 12's healing,** you've journeyed through raw pain, bitter honesty, spiritual prescription, and finally — hope.

This book was never about pretending divorce doesn't hurt; it was about showing that God heals what hurts, redeems what's broken, and writes fresh chapters when we think the story is over.

📋 Faith Clinic Discharge Plan

Patient Name: [Insert Yours Here]
Diagnosis: Survived Divorce. Healing in Progress. Hope Restored.
Attending Physician: The Great Healer (a.k.a. God)
Date of Discharge: Today. Yes, today.

Condition Upon Release

- No longer defined by failure.

- Walking in forgiveness and fresh identity.

- Capable of joy again without guilt.

- Spiritually stable, emotionally recovering, and purpose driven.

💊 PRESCRIPTIONS

1. **Daily Grace Capsule** — Take **Romans 8:1** every morning: *There is now no condemnation for those who are in Christ Jesus."*

2. **Hope Injections** — Administer **Psalm 147:3** daily: *He heals the brokenhearted and binds up their wounds."*

3. **Peace Tonic** — Breathe in **Philippians 4:6–7** when anxiety flares up.

4. **Forgiveness Ointment** — Apply generously to yourself and your ex, even when the scar itches.

5. **Identity Vitamins** — Repeat this daily: *I am loved, chosen, and not forgotten."*

Follow-Up Appointments

- **Prayer Check-Ups:** Meet with God daily (He never overbooks).

- **Word Therapy:** Read one Scripture per day that reminds you of identity, not shame.

- **Community Care:** Surround yourself with safe, faith-filled people.

- **Kingdom Assignment Review:** Ask God regularly: *What do You want me to build now?"*

⚠ WARNING SIGNS

Call your Physician immediately (yes, God answers 911 prayers) if you notice:

- Bitterness trying to settle in.

- Shame rehearsing lies on repeat.

- Hopelessness whispering "you'll never be happy again."

- Comparison scrolling through Instagram highlight reels of couples.

🍴 DIETARY INSTRUCTIONS

- Avoid steady meals of regret and "what ifs."

- Cut out overfeeding on old text messages and photos.

- Stay nourished with gratitude, worship, and future-focused conversations.

ACTIVITY GUIDELINES

- Resume living — joy is allowed.

- Move forward at your own pace — healing is not a sprint.

- Engage in Kingdom work — your purpose didn't file for divorce.

- Rest when needed — even Jesus napped.

FINAL WORDS FROM YOUR HEALER

"I know the plans I have for you," declares the Lord, *plans to prosper you and not to harm you, plans to give you hope and a future."* (**Jeremiah 29:11**)

This wasn't the end. It was the turning point. You're discharged not just to survive but to thrive.

Next Steps: Your Choice

- **Option A:** Keep reliving the past until bitterness makes you sick again.

- **Option B:** Leave this clinic with wholeness, walk in your healing, and live like someone who believes God still writes redemption stories.

Patient officially released.

Go in peace, live in purpose, and never forget: the same God who saw you through the courtroom will carry you into the calling room.

Faith Clinic Appointment Reminder Card

Patient: [Insert Your Name Here]
Next Appointment: Daily — God doesn't cancel.
Location: Prayer Closet / Kitchen Table / Car Ride / Anywhere You'll Actually Show Up.
Provider: Dr. Alpha & Omega, M.D. (Miracle Dealer).

Daily Check-Up Plan

- **Morning Dose:** Wake up and thank God you survived what tried to kill you.

- **Midday Boost:** Whisper "Boy, Bye" to bitterness and keep it moving.

- **Evening Refills:** Forgive yourself before bed — insomnia is not a ministry.

Don't Forget To Bring:

- An honest heart (fake faith gets no coverage).

- Your Bible (still the best prescription refill on the market).

- A willingness to heal (God won't drag you, He'll lead you).

Warning:

Missing appointments may cause relapse into pettiness, stalking your ex's Instagram, or thinking God canceled your future.

Next Visit Notes:

- Healing is ongoing, not one-and-done.

- Your divorce was not the expiration date on your destiny.

- Jesus is the ultimate rebound — and yes, He actually answers texts.

✒ **Signature:** _____

(*Reminder: The Physician already signed your future in blood on Calvary.*)

☑ See you at your daily check-in.

God's calendar is wide open, and He actually wants to hear from you.

Faith Clinic Prescription Pad

Patient Name: _____

Date: _____

Diagnosis: Survived Divorce (Symptoms: heartbreak, bitterness, overthinking, scrolling your ex's feed, pretending you're fine).

Prescribed By: The Great Physician (Dr. Jesus Christ, DDS — *Deliverer, Defender, Savior*).

Medication Orders:

- **Take 1 dose of Scripture daily** *(Example: **Psalm 34:18** — "The Lord is close to the brokenhearted and saves those who are crushed in spirit.")*

- **Pray with food, without food, or while eating ice cream straight from the carton.**

- **Repeat forgiveness until bitterness is no longer your bedtime snack.**

Refills:

- Unlimited. Covered by the Blood.

- No co-pay required. Grace has already been paid in full.

Side Effects:

- Increased peace.

- Sudden joy at random times (warning: you might laugh again).

- Reduced anxiety when you finally block their number.

- Hope that annoys people who expected you to stay broken.

Doctor's Notes:

- Healing starts in the spirit before it shows up in the flesh.

- Your story doesn't end with papers stamped by a judge.

- Destiny wasn't canceled — it was just redirected.

- Next appointment? Daily. Don't ghost your Healer.

Patient To-Do List:

1. Write down one Scripture you'll "swallow whole" today:
   _____

2. Write down one lie you'll evict (ex: "I'll never be loved again"): _____

3. Write down one truth you'll repeat until it sticks:
   _____

4. Write down one thing you forgive yourself for:
   _____

💊 FINAL REMINDER:

God's Word works if you take it. Stop leaving your medicine bottle on the nightstand unopened.

▉ Faith Clinic Journal Reflection Page

(Because sometimes you need to write it down before you throw it away — literally.)

Today's Date: _____

Prompt 1: Boy, Bye Moments

- Write down the exact moment you realized it was over (spiritually or physically).

- Be honest. Don't church it up.

- *Example:* "The divorce was done in year 2, I just stayed for year 20 because my mom told me 'God hates divorce.' Spoiler: God also hates me pretending I'm fine."

✍ Reflection:

_____

_____

_____

_____

_____

_____

_____

_____

Prompt 2: God in the Middle of the Mess

- Where did you feel Him?

- Was it through Scripture, a song, a friend, or the awkward silence after court?

- Don't say "nowhere" — He was there. Look again.

🕊 Reflection:

_____

_____

_____

_____

_____

_____

_____

_____

_____

_____

_____

_____

_____

Prompt 3: What I Forgive (Even If My Flesh Still Wants Revenge)

- Write one thing you're forgiving your ex for.

- Write one thing you're forgiving yourself for.

- Forgiveness ≠ amnesia. Forgiveness = eviction notice for bitterness.

🕊 Reflection:

_____

_____

_____

_____

_____

_____

_____

_____

_____

_____

_____

_____

_____

Prompt 4: My Faith Prescription

- Which Scripture will be your medicine this week?

- Example: **"Isaiah 43:19** — See, I am doing a new thing!"

- Write it. Pray it. Tape it to your fridge if you must.

Reflection:

_____

_____

_____

_____

_____

_____

_____

_____

_____

_____

_____

_____

Prompt 5: My "Amen" Future

- Imagine the next chapter.

- No more "if only." No more "I'll never."

- What new thing can God do in your life if you hand Him the pen?

✎ Reflection:

_____

_____

_____

_____

_____

_____

_____

_____

_____

✐ Closing Note:

This isn't just venting on paper — it's partnering with the Author of your story. Your "Boy, Bye" doesn't end with bitterness. It ends with "Amen." Because the court closed one chapter, but heaven is still writing the sequel.

"You don't have to be fully healed to keep breathing—you just have to be willing to move, even if it's with a limp. God walks with the wounded."

-DR. PATRICIA S. TANNER

ABOUT THE AUTHOR

Dr. Patricia Tanner was born and raised in Sanford FL. She comes from a family of three siblings. Patricia Tanner is the founder of Multhai International Realty, Multhai Asset Management Services, and Multhai Investment Group which is located in Sanford, Florida. She is a graduate of the University of Central Florida, where she received a Bachelor of Science in Business Administration and a minor in Human Resources Management.

Dr. Tanner began her career shortly thereafter as a Regional Property Manager in the apartment community. Throughout her career in property management, she has built interpersonal relationships with corporate clients. She has a successful track record of increasing company revenues over $5 million annually, through hard work, commitment, creativeness, and strategic planning.

Her experience and leadership role eventually led her to achieve a Florida Real Estate Broker license. She spent fifteen years in the Real Estate field while completing a Master of Arts in Human Resources Management from Webster University, and a Master of Public Administration from Troy University. It was in this capacity that she decided to open her own brokerage company, Multhai International Realty.

In addition, Dr. Tanner finds time in her busy schedule to participate in her own Non-For-Profit Organization, Stones 2 Homes. She remains President of her organization in which she helps people build, keep, or purchase homes in affordable communities. She is the founder of PNT Property Partners in which she buys vacant land, develops it, and constructs brand new construction homes in Sanford Florida. Her overall goal is to educate and provide resources to help people overcome financial hardships and credit disadvantage to live the American Dream through homeownership in spite of economic hardship. Through her visions she will continue to grow as an entrepreneur and is willing to share her knowledge, experience, and expertise with anyone who is willing to learn.

MORE BOOKS BY THE AUTHOR

Welcome to the Faith Clinic—where your soul doesn't need to be perfect to be healed.

You've smiled through burnout. Quoted scripture while quietly unraveling. Prayed, fasted, and still felt like your faith flatlined. If that's you, Faith Clinic: Volume I is your spiritual prescription.

Dr. Patricia S. Tanner—known as The Faith Doctor—invites you into a raw, grace-filled recovery journey for the soul. With 7 powerful doses of faith-infused wisdom, this book delivers healing where performance failed and offers truth where church hurt left a scar. Designed especially for spiritually exhausted youth and young adults, each "dose" reads like an IV drip of hope for believers secretly running on empty.

You don't need to be okay to show up. You just need to be willing. The clinic is open.

NOW AVAILABLE:
www.amazon.com

Healing was just the beginning. Now it's time to grow.

If Faith Clinic Volume I met you in crisis, Volume II meets you in recovery. Because faith isn't a one-time fix—it's a lifestyle that needs maintenance, accountability, and consistency. Welcome to your follow-up care plan.

In Faith Clinic: Volume II, Dr. Patricia S. Tanner—aka The Faith Doctor—guides you through the next level of your spiritual healing journey. From navigating church trauma and burnout to facing silence from God and rediscovering purpose, this book goes deeper than devotionals. It's not about hype—it's about habits that sustain real, lasting transformation.

With raw wisdom, relatable stories, and no-shame truths, each chapter is a spiritual check-in for believers who want to thrive—not just survive. Whether you're wrestling with doubt, craving stability, or simply ready to grow up in God, this clinic is for you.

You've detoxed. Now it's time to build. Let's get you discharge-ready.

NOW AVAILABLE:
www.amazon.com

Welcome to the Faith Clinic: Anxiety Edition — where God doesn't coddle your coping mechanisms but confronts them with surgical precision.

This book is for the ones who love Jesus but still can't sleep. For the worship leaders crying in church bathrooms. For the believers who pray in spirals, fight shame on Sundays, and secretly think, "Maybe I'm the only one who can't seem to breathe through this." You're not crazy. You're just in a fight — and this book is your spiritual triage.

Inside you'll find:
☑ Panic attacks in pews and the prayers that still work.
☑ Scriptures that talk you off the ledge.
☑ What to do when you feel numb and God feels quiet.
☑ How to walk out of shame loops, judgment spirals, and performance religion.

This isn't just encouragement. It's equipment.
Because healing isn't a moment — it's a walk.

NOW AVAILABLE:
www.amazon.com

Welcome to the Faith Clinic: Stress Edition — where we don't hand you cute verses and clichés. We hand you spiritual prescriptions for real pressure, real panic, and real prayers from tired believers holding it together by a thread.

This book is for the overwhelmed—those trusting God while juggling bills, burnout, hustle culture, and holy frustration. If you've ever whispered, "God, are You even watching this mess?" this is for you.

Inside you'll find raw, soul-hitting chapters like:

- "God, I Trust You — But These Bills Keep Coming"
- "If Rest Is Holy, Why Does It Feel Like Slacking?"
- "I'm Tired of Smiling So You Won't Worry"

This isn't fluff. It's real talk for real stress—and a reminder that you're not forgotten, you're being fortified.

The Faith Clinic is open. Breathe in & take your spiritual vitamins. Healing begins here.

NOW AVAILABLE:
www.amazon.com

This isn't just a feeling — it's a flare signal from the soul. You pray, serve, and believe in God, but something deep inside is still simmering. Welcome to the Faith Clinic: Anger Edition — where suppressed emotions meet sacred intervention.

In this volume, Dr. Patricia S. Tanner guides you through spiritual triage for:

☑ Silent rage and emotional suppression

☑ The grief–anger connection

☑ Rejection wounds from childhood to church hurt

This isn't a lecture. It's a spiritual detox. No shame. No sugar-coating. Just raw, honest healing. Whether you're snapping at loved ones or silently seething under the surface, this book meets you at the boiling point—and leads you to the breakthrough.

⚕ This is the clinic.

◍ This is your moment.

And God is ready to heal the anger behind your amen.

NOW AVAILABLE:
www.amazon.com

In this powerful installment of the Faith Clinic series, Dr. Patricia S. Tanner brings biblical insight, emotional compassion, and spiritual strength to those walking through grief. Designed as a healing chamber for the soul, each "dose" of this devotional targets a different dimension of sorrow—guiding you from pain to peace, from mourning to joy.

Inside, you'll discover:

- Daily doses of Scripture-based encouragement.
- Personal reflections and prayers for each stage of grief.
- Practical faith prescriptions to help you process loss and find purpose.

Whether you are navigating the recent loss of a loved one, confronting buried grief from the past, or supporting someone else in their sorrow, this devotional offers a gentle yet powerful roadmap to healing. Come, take your seat in the Faith Clinic—where the Great Physician is ready to restore your soul.

NOW AVAILABLE:
www.amazon.com

30 Days Of Grieving

Given By The Inspiration Of God

Healing From COVID-19

Almost a year later, it hit me... My mother was gone, and I was still stuck at the hospital. I had tried everything from crying to counseling, and even prayer. Pray they told me. Trust God they insisted. But it seemed as if nothing was working. I was hurt, dealing with my reality: my mother was not coming back.

While journeying through grief, it was under the divine 'Inspiration of God' that He placed me in a trance. While I was gaining a revelation about grief, He gave me this journal, '30 Days Of Grieving.'

NOW AVAILABLE:
www.amazon.com

The 30 Days Challenge:
I Tested POSITIVE for COVID-19

If you had 30 days to live, what would you do? If you were told that you needed to prepare for a marathon in 30 days and you were completely out of shape, what would you do first? If a family member handed you one million dollars and told you that you had to figure out how to build a house (debt free), how would you execute your plan?

I'm catching you off guard with these requests, right? Well, this is exactly what COVID-19 did when it snatched my mother's life away, wrecking my entire world. I had to battle for my mother AND my faith in 30 days flat. What a challenge!

Throughout this book, I will walk you through my brief journey with COVID-19, negative of a happy ending. I will share the diary I kept while attending to my mother, and the scriptures I read, prayed, and quoted as my shield and protection.

Take the journey with me, there is healing on the other side!

NOW AVAILABLE:
www.amazon.com

Can Salvation Get You Into Heaven? The Answer Is Yes! offers a powerful and biblically grounded exploration of God's eternal plan, revealing the heart of the Gospel and the assurance of salvation through Jesus Christ.

 Unpacking life's most vital questions—Who is God? Why were we created? What does Jesus' life mean for us?—this book brings clarity to the believer's journey and confirms that salvation, once received, is eternally secure.

Whether you're seeking understanding or affirming your faith, this inspiring guide will lead you into the confidence and joy of knowing heaven is your eternal home.

NOW AVAILABLE:

www.amazon.com

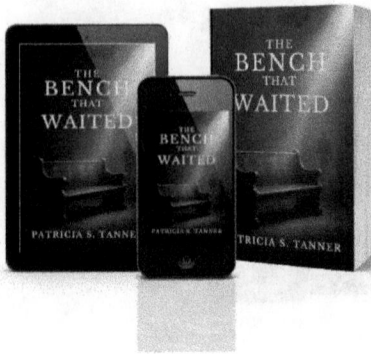

The Bench That Waited is a bold and prophetic call to action for believers who've grown comfortable in church attendance but stagnant in purpose.

With raw honesty and spiritual insight, Patricia Tanner exposes the quiet crisis of passive faith—where callings are delayed and obedience is optional.

Through Scripture, stories, and reflection, this book urges readers to rise from routine, break free from spiritual stagnation, and step boldly into their Kingdom assignment. The bench has waited long enough—will you?

NOW AVAILABLE:
www.amazon.com

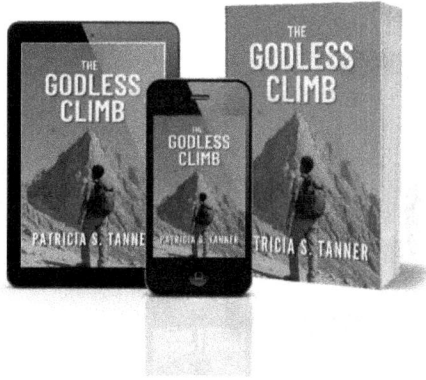

What happens when the Kingdom becomes a stranger?

The Godless Climb is not a rejection of faith—it is a raw, unflinching journey through what remains when belief unravels. With brutal honesty and tender grace, this book explores the spiritual free fall that follows the loss of divine certainty, the ache of unanswered prayers, and the void left when God no longer feels near.

Written for those who have quietly slipped out of the pews and into a wilderness of doubt, grief, and inner searching, this is not a triumph story—but a survival story. A confession. A sacred wrestle. Through personal reflection and prophetic insight, the author unpacks what it means to climb without a safety net, to live without the scaffolding of religious performance, and to build a new compass in the absence of old crutches.

You haven't arrived. But you're still climbing. And that is holy.

NOW AVAILABLE:
www.amazon.com

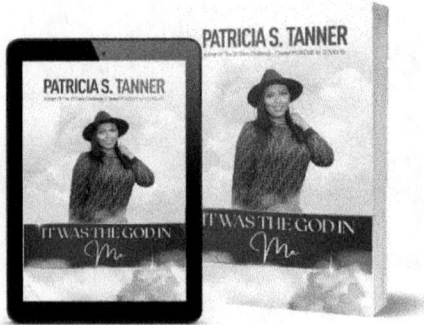

It Was The God In

Success can be attributed to many things. Depending on the person who has obtained success would determine those to whom they attribute their success. Some give credit to their daily routine while others give credit to a mentor or some sort of system they followed. When I think about my success, the only person who I can give the credit to is God.

In this memoir, I share the successes and failures I have experienced throughout my life. From my individual experiences to my entrepreneurial journey, I share how God has walked with me every step of the way.

Come and see.. It Was The God In Me!!

NOW AVAILABLE:
www.amazon.com

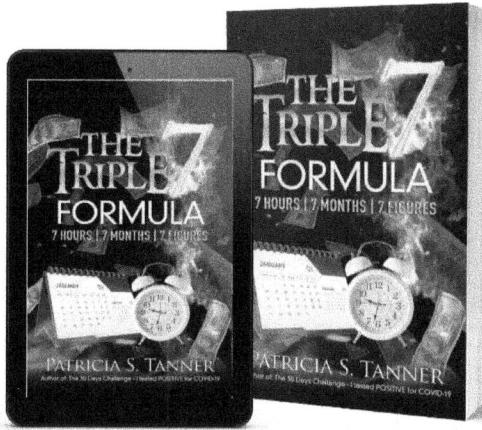

The Triple 7 Formula is designed for business owners who are looking forward to hitting the million-dollar mark in their business. If you own a business and seem to be running in financial circles, this book will get you on track to simultaneously gaining sound business structure and millions in your bank account.

It was through many conversations with business owners lacking financial gain that prompted Patricia to share her blueprint for millionaire status. Through this book, she demonstrates how to gain financial ground by developing strong teams, implementing systems, and setting stackable goals. If you are ready to gain a laser sharp focus, and implement these clear steps, you will position yourself for financial greatness. Your business will be sound, and you will see financial growth beyond your wildest dreams!!

NOW AVAILABLE:
www.amazon.com

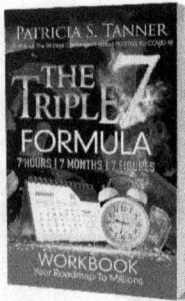

The Triple 7 Formula is specifically crafted for business owners aspiring to reach the million-dollar milestone. If you are a business owner feeling stuck in financial cycles, this book will set you on the path to building both a solid business structure and financial success.

This workbook is designed to complement the textbook of the same name. As you progress through its pages, you will be inspired to take decisive steps toward becoming a millionaire. From constructing your business framework to creating the millionaire's avatar, this process will expand your knowledge and mindset. Not only will you chart a course to financial success, but you will also identify your accountability circle and select a mentor to guide you toward greatness.

I cannot guarantee millionaire status unless you actively follow the steps to begin your journey. If you are searching for a get rich quick scheme, this workbook is not for you. I am looking for those ready to put in the effort—and since you are reading this, I believe that's you!

You have finally found it: Your roadmap to millions!

NOW AVAILABLE:
WWW.Amazon.com

Find Patricia on The Web:

www.PatriciaTanner.com

Follow Patricia on social media:

Facebook & Instagram: @PatriciaTannerInc

DR. PATRICIA S. TANNER

www.ingramcontent.com/pod-product-compliance
Lightning Source LLC
Chambersburg PA
CBHW062216080426
42734CB00010B/1912